The Snake that Swallowed Its Tail

For Millie, as a token of excessive and probably counter-productive parental expectations.

The Snake that Swallowed Its Tail

Mark Garnett

ia

IMPRINT ACADEMIC

Published in the UK by Imprint Academic
PO Box 200, Exeter EX5 5YX, UK

Published in the USA by Imprint Academic
Philosophy Documentation Center
PO Box 7147, Charlottesville, VA 22906-7147, USA

ISBN 0 907845 88 6

A CIP catalogue record for this book is available from the
British Library and US Library of Congress

Contents

Acknowledgements   6

Introduction   7

The Anatomy of a Snake   13

The Media   31

Politics   51

The Public Services   73

Bibliography   94

Societas: Essays in political and cultural criticism   96

Acknowledgements

Nick Cohen, John Hoffman and Ivo Mosley kindly read parts of this essay in the early stages of drafting. Keith Sutherland read the whole manuscript and has offered friendly encouragement throughout. I am most grateful to these friends for their helpful suggestions, and to Keith for his insights into the work of Edward Hopper. But in respect of any errors of fact or interpretation in what follows I must obey the precepts of liberal individualism and accept full responsibility.

Introduction

After the destruction of the World Trade Center in September 2001, Western political leaders agreed that the terrorists had attacked everything their civilisation stood for. When they recited their list of threatened values, the same words and phrases turned up again and again: democracy, freedom of speech, tolerance, etc. Although the ruling parties in different countries bore a variety of names, under the pressure of events they had lined up to claim membership of the same ideological family. The values they named were all highly characteristic of liberalism.

The claim that liberalism is the presiding spirit in Western politics and society will be familiar to most students of ideology. John Gray, for example, has written that liberalism is 'the political theory of modernity'.[1] According to Richard Bellamy, 'From New Right Conservatives to democratic socialists, it seems that we are all liberals now'.[2] Anyone who doubts these judgements should remember that over the past two centuries Western states have adopted the procedures of liberal democracy — the ones which, we are told, were attacked on September 11. Those procedures have not become prevalent throughout the West by accident, but because of the success of liberal ideas. And since we operate within a framework of liberal institutions, it is hardly surprising that we have also adopted the vocabulary of liberalism. Political parties across the West have come to resemble each other — both within and across national boundaries. But the

---

[1]   John Gray, *Liberalism*, Open University, 1986, 82.
[2]   Richard Bellamy, *Liberalism and Modern Society*, Polity Press, 1992, 1.

influence of liberalism has extended far beyond politics. It informs even the mundane activities of the lives we lead within a liberal economic order.

However, events since September 11 have demonstrated that a liberal consensus is no guarantee of unanimity, even on issues of fundamental principle. People with impeccable liberal credentials have argued passionately on both sides of the case for war on Iraq. In Britain, tough new anti-terrorist laws have been introduced, the right to trial by jury is under threat, and before long we are likely to be issued with identity cards. Some critics have accused New Labour of deserting the liberal stance it adopted in opposition. In reply, the government insists that it is only taking the necessary steps to preserve a liberal society through a time of crisis. As a reliable press supporter has argued, 'Better a five-minute wait or an ID card than a bomb'.[3]

Important though they are, these debates are not the central concern of this essay. I want to remind readers that a schism could be detected in liberal ranks long before September 2001. I call the rival camps 'fleshed-out' and 'hollowed-out' liberalism. The former retains a close resemblance to the ideas of the greatest liberal thinkers, who were optimistic about human nature and envisaged a society made up of free, rational individuals, respecting themselves and others. The latter, by contrast, satisfies no more than the basic requirements of liberal thought. It reduces the concepts of reason and individual fulfilment to the lowest common denominator, identifying them with the pursuit of short-term material self-interest. For the hollowed-out liberal, other people are either means to an end, or obstacles which must be shunted aside. Instead of an equality of respect, this is more like equality of contempt. But from the point of view of liberal theory, all that really matters is that other people are treated *equally*.[4]

When we say that liberalism is dominant in the West, I believe that we are referring to this hollow form. It is the presiding spirit of the media, which shapes so much of our thinking even if we

[3]   Peter Riddell in the *Times*, 8 April 2004.
[4]   This, of course, is not to be confused with the socialist ideal of equalising economic outcomes.

are often unconscious of its effects. The advertising industry would collapse without it. Increasingly it provides political debate with its underlying assumptions. And its influence over society as a whole can only come at the expense of the fleshed-out version. Those who try to organise their lives around long-term expectations find it hard to cling to their views when they think that people around them are driven by the desire for immediate gratification. Unless they possess unusual resolve, they will have to act in accordance with the prevailing mood; and experience will sap them of the optimism which is essential to their beliefs. It only requires a few concrete examples of hypocrisy and deceit to make us wary of new acquaintances; and, in time, we even begin to worry about the motivations of our 'nearest and dearest'. Thus the success of hollowed-out liberalism has a tendency to reinforce itself. Social life becomes a series of tentative encounters, and white-collar work consists of dreary routine punctuated by fruitless bonding sessions.

Some argue that the triumph of hollow liberalism is inevitable. It seems highly appropriate for fast-changing times, characterised by economic and emotional insecurity. In recent years we have indeed seen the emergence of a new hollow vocabulary — management-speak, political correctness, and the various discourses of 'choice'. But Westerners need more than this. More than ever, they are searching for reassurance that they are right as well as rich. After 9/11, their politicians were forced to address this question. Despite the feverish atmosphere of the time, they still sounded unconvincing as they testified to the glories of Western civilisation. It was too obvious that there was a mismatch between the panegyric and its object. Their slogans were borrowed from the great tradition of fleshed-out liberalism; but they were using them to praise hollow societies.

Rather than being a convenient counterpart to a consumerist society, hollowed-out liberalism is beginning to look like an unsavoury relic of the Cold War. Until the collapse of the Communist bloc, Western leaders could afford to talk in clichés because they knew that the 'battle of ideas' was being decided by economic growth-rates. Ronald Reagan and Margaret Thatcher got away with it; but George W. Bush and Tony Blair are fighting a very different war, which cannot be won without a meaningful moral vision. It will be some time before another British political party embarks on a dubious war after blabbering on about the 'ethical dimension' to its foreign policy.

Bush and Blair are also fighting their war in a different context. In Britain we have just celebrated twenty-five years of hire-and-fire capitalism. It has survived almost as long as the 'mixed economy' which preceded it. Although the pace of contemporary life is a deterrent to serious reflection, there is evidence that many people are beginning to take stock. Even if we accept that the philosophy of selfishness has played a significant role in boosting average living standards in the West, our relative success in this sphere has given us a unique opportunity to wonder if selfishness is all that life has to offer. It provides us with the chance to see that hollowed-out liberalism is more than just a libel on human nature. It is also contradictory and self-defeating. It can only find a semblance of moral justification in ideas and slogans which rightly belong to an older and better tradition. The more often we hear them, the more we recognise that they are being taken out of their proper context.

This is a polemical essay, not a systematic treatise. It is not the place to attempt a complete explanation of our current predicament. My objective is simply to point out some of the contradictions of hollowed-out liberalism, as they are beginning to affect British society. I argue that this form of liberalism is like the snake which tried to swallow its tail. It is doomed by its combination of insulting presuppositions about human nature, and an inability to look beyond short-term interests. Its internal logic makes it grasp at expedients which only make things worse. Thus senior politicians respond to voter apathy with spin, sound-bites and slurs on their opponents. Newspaper editors worried about falling circulation dig deeper into the private lives of celebrities, eroding public interest in the celebrity culture which provides them with most of their 'news'. And in their quest to ensnare the hollow viewer, television executives commission a stream of 'reality' programmes which prove that reality in a hollow society is irredeemably tedious and unwatchable.

Things are likely to get worse before they improve, but I believe that the snake of hollowed-out liberalism is coming towards the end of its last meal. The rate of ingestion has certainly been increasing, and the gap between rhetoric and reality is now too glaring to ignore. In case the reader thinks that this perception is the product of wishful thinking on my part, I should explain that I have serious reservations about *both* forms of liberalism. I do not think that the disappearance of the snake will be followed by the enthronement of fleshed-out rationality and a new age of mutual respect. I am a partisan in this matter because I believe that a liberal society which bears a closer approximation to its stated principles is the best practicable option in our present circumstances. The only imaginable alternative is some kind of authoritarian regime. The longer we allow our elected leaders and self-appointed oracles to persist with their hollow assumptions about human nature, the more likely we are to lose the form as well as the substance of a liberal society.

Some readers might find the present argument excessively parochial. Hollowed-out liberalism might not have swept over the whole world, but since the end of the Cold War it has made significant advances from its North American and Western European heartlands. If it seems on the point of destroying itself over here, we might expect to trace similar developments in other countries. We could, for example, take a critical look at the attempts to engraft liberalism in the former countries of the Soviet bloc; the abuse of human rights at Guantanamo Bay; or the assault on a pluralist media conducted by Tony Blair's intimate friend, Signor Berlusconi. What about the phenomenon of 'globalisation', which has drawn diverse groups into a struggle once monopolised by Marxists? And there must be room for an account of climate change, which hollowed-out liberals are trying to address by using lead-free petrol on their unnecessary car journeys. Surely this is the biggest contradiction of all, in which consumerist individualism is doing its best to ensure that there will soon be no living individuals?

The scope of the essay does not allow for detailed consideration of these issues. Although it has a fairly narrow focus, I hope that it develops some arguments which have a bearing on the larger questions. Above all, it is a challenge to fleshed-out liberals who must be feeling confused and beaten in the Britain of today. Western liberalism really is under attack: but its half-faced friends are more dangerous than its avowed enemies. When the snake finally swallows its tail we will depend on the true believers to throw off their lethargy and step into the void.

Chapter 1

The Anatomy
of a Snake

> I'm becoming heartily sick of liberalism. It's complicated, and tiring, and open to misrepresentation and abuse by ... by sneaky, spoiled children. And it breeds doubt, and I'm sick of doubt, too; I want certitude...

Katie Carr, the central character in Nick Hornby's novel *How to be Good* (2001), is facing a spiritual crisis. Her husband, previously a snarling cynic, has suddenly become a sanctimonious saint; but domestic harmony is as distant as ever. Katie is also a doctor in general practise, which (as we shall see) gives her special reasons for feeling undervalued and unworthy by turns. Her behaviour in response to these troubles is fairly predictable; she has an unsatisfactory sexual dalliance, quarrels with her children and questions the point of it all.

But if Katie's disorder is nothing out of the ordinary, her diagnosis is a nasty surprise. Nowadays, to be sick of liberalism is to be tired of life. Britain is a liberal democracy, and so are all the other countries we respect. We still have different party labels, but these are merely souvenirs from a receding time when socialists and conservatives (of a kind) roamed the earth. The influence of values like democracy and free speech extends far beyond politics, pervading every significant aspect of our lives. And the impact has extended far beyond the West. A decade ago a widely-discussed book told us that the world-wide triumph of liberalism had put an end to history[1]. The verdict has proved slightly premature. But recalcitrant regions of the globe are now being taught appropriate lessons, to ensure that nothing of historical interest happens again. Even we could do with a refresher course, apparently. Jonathan Freedland of the *Guardian* has lamented that although British writers were largely responsible for the development of liberalism, the country has yet to enjoy its full fruits. He urges us to Bring Home the Revolution, so that Britain Can Live the American Dream (or something broadly similar, leaving out the bits which even Freedland finds disagreeable).[2] Fittingly, his book appeared in the year that Britain absorbed the European Convention of Human Rights into its domestic law, thus 'bringing home' the list of well-meaning and contradictory sentiments which our representatives helped to compile in 1950.

It would be comforting to think that Katie is attacking the wrong target, having mistaken the real nature of liberalism. She admits freely that her own beliefs are 'complicated ... open to misinterpretation and abuse'. If she is confused, she wouldn't be alone. Ideological terms tend to be very confusing indeed. Even in Mr Freedland's Land of Dreams, the United States, there are people who have yet to comprehend the nature of the values that give their country its improbable sense of unity. Right-wing Republicans who call themselves 'conservatives' subject 'liberals' to humourless and ill-informed abuse on talk radio. If 'liberal' tendencies can be exposed in a Democratic presidential candidate, even an incumbent with an indefensible record can hope to be re-elected. In Britain, supporters of the Conservative Party equate liberalism with 'do-gooders', '*Guardian* readers', or

---

[1]   Francis Fukuyama, *The End of History and The Last Man*, Penguin edition, 1992. Now that people have stopped talking about Fukuyama's book, they should actually read it. Apart from his Big Prediction, they will find a host of little ironies. To take one at random: 'The days of Islam's cultural conquests, it would seem, are over' (p.46). Or perhaps some people did read Fukuyama after all; his assumption that Islamic fundamentalism is nothing more than a panic-stricken reaction from people who recognise the superiority of liberal ideas is certainly shared by members of the Bush administration.

[2]   Jonathan Freedland, *Bring Home the Revolution: How Britain Can Live the American Dream*, Fourth Estate, 1998.

members of the 'chattering classes' who are soft on the perpetrators of crime and tough on populist Home Secretaries. Whereas in the USA they are almost certain to be Democrats, in Britain liberals of this kind have given up on making a constructive impact through political parties; they are voluble complainers and habitual abstainers. On both sides of the Atlantic, the political right agrees that they would be glad to commit treason, if only they were a little braver. Even at times of real crisis, they insist upon questioning the superiority of the Western way of life — although few of them go so far as its spurn its material benefits.

In view of their differences, it seems odd to think of Katie and the hate-police of American talk radio as members of one very big, deeply unhappy liberal family. But liberalism is as remarkable for its divisions as for its dominance. Whatever they might think, in Britain and the USA self-professed 'conservatives' are actually liberals in denial.[3] Their fanatical support for free market ideas is largely responsible for the social evils that they stigmatise, but they are far too short-sighted to make the connection. They agree with Tony Blair in blaming everything on the 1960s. By contrast, people like Katie are liberals who pore over the pages of the *Guardian* in the hope of finding something to feel guilty about.

Why does it make sense to lump all these people into the 'liberal' category? Although there is room for endless dispute on the subject, for the present purpose we can identify four core liberal beliefs: that the individual ought to be treated as prior to society; that human beings are capable of rational decision-making; that rational people are worthy of equal respect; and that freedom is the best guarantee of individual fulfilment. We might think that this is no more than a list of common-sense propositions. But that would only show how far we have absorbed liberalism into ourselves, for 'common sense' is a relative concept, reserved for ideas which we take for granted even though others might find them bizarre. Freedland is right: British authors were indeed the first to provide a systematic exposition of liberal ideas. However, beyond this he is radically wrong. There was never any

---

[3]   As opposed to conservatives being liberals who have been mugged.

need for us to 'bring home the revolution'. Unlike our manufac-
turing industry, this was one innovation we kept hold of. Until
fairly recently we have just been a bit slow in working through
all of its implications.

So what, exactly, are these implications? One of the problems
with liberalism is that you can't know what you've bargained for
until you've signed for the full delivery; and then it's too late to
go back. The difficulties of definition only crop up after the triumph of the liberal revolution is complete, and the last pockets
of ideological resistance are being mopped up. At that point
terms like 'reason', 'individual fulfilment', 'respect' and even
'freedom', which sounded straightforward and very appealing
when liberalism was primarily a language of protest, turn out to
be pretty elusive. Thus many of us will agree with Katie in thinking that 'rational' behaviour includes some consideration for
others; we feel, like her, that life cannot be truly fulfilling unless
one has made a reasonable effort on their behalf. We recognise
that we get some private satisfaction from helping out. We do
not claim to act out of unadulterated altruism. But we are not so
simple- minded as to confuse our motives with downright selfishness. We recognise the difference between the feeling which
arises from successful attempts to help others and the pleasure
which selfish people feel when they help themselves.[4]

But we are well aware that other people reach very different
conclusions from the same liberal premises. Before his improbable conversion, Katie's husband was a journalist whose only reliable source of income was a newspaper column ('The Angriest
Man in Holloway') which focused with some relish on friction
between different members of society. Thus he satisfied the four
liberal criteria: he thought in terms of individuals rather than
society; he exploited the freedom to say what he liked; he had no
more respect for his readers than his victims; and his outlook
was rational because it made him money. He could readily
assume that this version of liberalism was widely shared, at least

---

[4]   Although this idiotic confusion of terms was exploded by Bishop Butler in
       the eighteenth century, he could have spared himself the labour. Almost
       everyone nowadays seems to assume that selfishness and self-love are the
       same thing.

in Holloway; otherwise market forces would have forced his editor to stop commissioning his diatribes.

Ironically, Katie's husband underpinned her moral universe when he allowed his malevolent media alter ego to intrude upon his private life. Whenever they disagreed, she could be fairly sure that she was right. But after his transformation he begins to give away their children's possessions to needy neighbours, and her admiration for his new-style 'certitude' is no match for her feeling that he is making himself look ridiculous. By taking her own principles to their logical conclusion, he is subverting them by showing that they make no sense at all in the contemporary context. She even starts to wish for the return of his old sour self, treating everyone with contempt and urging that homeless people should be shot rather than offered accommodation. At least then she could go back to blaming him instead of facing up to her new sense of moral loneliness.

I shall argue in this essay that Katie's dilemma bears a striking resemblance to the underlying tensions of our own daily lives. Although we might want to act with a degree of consideration for others, even this inexacting standard requires nourishment from reciprocal relationships; we need to feel that we belong to a community of kindred spirits. This comforting feeling has been lost to all but a very fortunate few. At best, we are now uncertain of the motivations of those around us — all but our closest friends and relatives. More often, we find ourselves adopting the working assumption that everyone we meet — including even those 'friends' and relatives — is inherently short-sighted and selfish. We have room in our world-view for unselfish acts, even celebrating the most spectacular examples in our tabloid newspapers: but only so long as they are isolated instances. If we meet someone who behaves consistently like Katie's husband in his benevolent phase, we think either that they are insane or that their behaviour is an unconvincing mask for some ulterior motive. We are even beginning to share the delight of the tabloid press when it exposes the frailties of people with moral pretensions.

We have ended up facing Katie's dilemma because of the nature of the dominant message we receive, from the media,

from advertising and (as I shall argue) increasingly from politicians whose choice of career should imply that they know better.
In trivial details these voices might conflict, but for practical pur-
poses they resolve themselves into a single viewpoint — a uniform assumption that 'rational' conduct is synonymous with the
pursuit of immediate self-interest. Its practical effect is reflected
in almost everything we do. It makes us work increasingly hard
to supply ourselves with diminishing leisure-time rewards. Our
worldly wisdom comes from the solitary consumption of soap-
operas and self-help manuals. We go out of our way to avoid
encounters with others, feeling happier even when our addiction to the motor-car leaves us stranded in interminable queues.[5]
In the process we are steadily accumulating negative social capi-
tal, gradually making life less satisfactory for anyone who
retains any hope that society could be informed by more elevated principles. In a grotesque parody of Keynesian economics,
we have generated a 'misery multiplier'. Momentary collisions
with unhappy, frustrated people produce the same emotions in
ourselves, and we go on to infect others in a geometrical progression.

And yet the procedures of the media, the free market, and representative democracy are increasingly difficult to contest. The
frontal challenge from Marxism has been washed away by Cold
War propaganda and the swamping of traditional social boundaries in Britain; even the advertisers have decided that we have
become a society of types rather than classes. Most people who
call themselves feminists are anxious to justify the crudest practices of consumer society. In its most radical form, environmen-
talism demands a revolutionary change in Western life-styles;
and for that very reason few are prepared to back their commitment with more than token gestures. Conservatism in Britain
was dying long before Margaret Thatcher hijacked the party of
that name and purged its senior ranks of ideological dissidents.

---

[5]   The Sony 'walkman' — a device which isolates oneself and irritates others
       — was introduced to Britain in the month after Mrs Thatcher became Prime
       Minister. It would be a slander on the company's marketing strategists if
       we were to mark this down as nothing more than a delicious coincidence
       (see Larry Elliott and Dan Atkinson, *The Age of Insecurity*, Verso, 1998, 53).

The only realistic chance of constructing a persuasive critique seems to lie with liberalism itself — that is, with the spirit which animated the great thinkers of the liberal tradition in previous centuries. If we can recover some of their intentions, we can draw some conclusions about their descendants. We might be able to show that, while most of us are liberals, some are a great deal more liberal than others.

Two Concepts of Liberalism

In each of his contrasting guises, Katie's husband reflects the most influential interpretation of modern liberalism. As a cynic, he rejects the idea that anything should be done to help the disadvantaged; as a saint, he thinks that everyone should be given something like an equal chance to live in a way which fulfils their potential as human beings. These positions are reminiscent of the 'negative' and 'positive' concepts of liberty, identified by Isaiah Berlin in his celebrated Oxford inaugural lecture (1958).[6] 'Negative' liberty equates freedom with the absence of obstacles deliberately imposed by other people. By contrast, on the 'positive' view, freedom is only meaningful to an individual who possesses certain attributes and resources. To take the most familiar illustration of Berlin's distinction, on the 'negative' concept of liberty we are all 'free' to dine at an exclusive restaurant, or to fly. These happy notions are contested by the advocate of 'positive' liberty, who notes that we can only dine out in style if we have enough money to settle the bill — or if we have the cunning and quickness of feet to leave without paying, since our lack of wings makes it meaningless to suggest that we might fly out of the restaurant. But for believers in positive liberty, attributes are more important than resources, although there is clearly a link between the two. Being free in the 'positive' sense is only possible for a certain type of person; and although desperate poverty is clearly a barrier to healthy character-development, nowadays the same is equally true of excessive riches.

---

[6]   Isaiah Berlin, 'Two Concepts of Liberty', in *Four Essays on Liberty*, Oxford University Press, 1969.

Berlin's dichotomy has proved very helpful for teachers of political ideas. It illuminates the key issue of twentieth century politics — how far, and on what grounds, should the state interfere in the lives of its citizens? It seems to explain a schism between some liberals — practitioners and theorists alike — who believe that the state should leave people alone, and others who urge that without a guarantee of resources such as education, health care and a basic income, 'freedom' will be reserved for the well-to-do. The obvious problem with using Berlin in this context is the fact that he skewed his argument, not so much in favour of 'negative' liberty as against the 'positive' variant, which he associated with coercion. Some (though not all) believers in positive liberty have exhibited a strange blend of optimism and pessimism: they think that people have a 'better self' which can be fostered, but concede that they might have to be 'forced' to acknowledge this truly 'rational' being within them. For Berlin, that was the first step in a journey towards the intellectual endorsement of full-blown totalitarianism. On the doubtful supposition that neither Hitler nor Stalin would have hurt a fly without the backing of a few obliging theorists, Berlin could make even a freedom-lover like Jean-Jacques Rousseau appear to be the unwitting assistant of these murderous dictators. His argument implied that even the kindly scholar T H Green had been secretly shod in jackboots.

The success of Berlin's lecture has had two regrettable effects. It tends to encourage a distorted understanding of the relationship between theory and practice; and it deflects attention from the actual intentions of the great liberal writers.[7] On the first point, Berlin was right to warn that 'primitive and unchecked political beliefs' can sometimes exercise a 'fatal power', and lead to 'devastating effects'. But the relevance of his argument to the Britain of 1958 was obscure. As far as the state was concerned,

---

[7]   The same is true, I would argue, of the current vogue for debating the differences between 'libertarians' and 'communitarians'. It may be that I am transgressing the boundaries between academic disciplines, and writing about liberalism as an ethical doctrine rather than a political or sociological creed. So much the worse, in my view, for academic disciplines.

the battle of ideas had already ended in a typical compromise, leaving both the 'negatives' and the 'positives' dissatisfied. As soon as the franchise was extended beyond the middle classes it was no longer realistic for politicians to embrace the crude laissez-faire theory suggested by the 'negative' view of liberty. But although the state extended its activities — provoking negative liberals like F.A. von Hayek to thunder on about an alleged 'Road to Serfdom' — it did so within definite limits. A redistributive income tax was now as inevitable as death, and partially financed a network of institutions which provided sustenance 'from the cradle to the grave'. But even before the reforms of the Thatcher era, the tax regime permitted accumulation beyond the conceivable needs of any individual; and the welfare state has always been limited enough to ensure that only the exploits of a criminal mastermind could guarantee a comfortable life on its proceeds. From about 1960 to the late 1970s governments became 'overloaded', taking on responsibilities for economic management which proved self-defeating. But attempts at economic planning were half-hearted, and instead of storming the 'commanding heights of the British economy' governments tried to salvage wrecks from the sea-bed. Meanwhile, continued private provision in education and health-care meant that, on the 'positive' definition, the affluent did enjoy the potential to become far more 'free' than the poor (so long as they were sensible enough to avoid the parallel pitfall of decadence).

But Berlin's lecture had nothing to do with practical realities in Britain. It was his little contribution to the Cold War effort.[8] Reminding intelligent readers that the road to hell is paved with good intentions was potentially a useful supplement to the work of cruder Western propagandists, who asserted that Marx's intentions were deplorable in the first place. Berlin extended the indictment beyond Marx, to liberal thinkers whose work might corrupt innocent minds in British universities. The timing was very useful in this context; the lecture was delivered two years after Anthony Crosland had published *The Future of Socialism*,

---

[8]   Or, in Hywel Williams's phrase, Berlin was 'the cultural representative of a CIA view of the world', *Guardian*, 14 May 2004.

which attempted to show that extensive state intervention in Britain could not destroy freedom because of the 'long liberal tradition' in this country.[9] Berlin begged to differ without illustrating his argument with a single example drawn from concrete experience in the UK.

Now that the Cold War is over, we can turn back to liberal thinkers and their intentions, rather than lavishing all our attention on a hypothetical argument about their practical results. Whatever they thought about the proper role for the state, they always regarded it as a means to an end — a way of achieving their ultimate objective, which was to promote their own ideas on the nature of individual fulfilment and the extent of human potential.[10] Viewed from this perspective, we get a different list from Berlin's goodies and baddies, the 'negatives' and the 'positives'. On one side are thinkers whose liberalism is 'fleshed-out', arguing that rationality adds up to something more than purblind selfishness even if it takes some effort for us to see this for ourselves. Almost every liberal writer of note — even Adam Smith, of misunderstood memory — has been inspired by this vision. The bluntest and best expression of this view comes from John Stuart Mill — 'better to be Socrates dissatisfied than a fool satisfied'.[11] If more recent examples are relatively scarce, this reflects the decline of political theory and a more general mood of pessimism among intellectuals. But during the Second World War Erich Fromm - a wiser opponent of totalitarianism than Berlin and Hayek — argued that freedom is 'the active and spontaneous realization of the individual self', and warned that liberty could not be trusted in the hands of underdeveloped human beings.[12]

These eloquent advocates of 'fleshed-out' liberty have been opposed by a handful of misanthropes, who think that everyone apart from themselves is swimming in a sewer of stupidity

[9]   Anthony Crosland, *The Future of Socialism*, abridged edition, Jonathan Cape, 1964, 177.
[10]   As David Selbourne puts it, the state was seen as an instrument of the 'soveriegn civic order'; see *The Principle of Duty*, Sinclair-Stevenson, 1994.
[11]   John Stuart Mill, 'Utilitarianism', in *Collected Works*, Vol X, *Essays on Ethics, Religion and Society*, Routledge & Kegan Paul, 1969, 212.
[12]   Erich Fromm, *Fear of Freedom* [1942], Routledge edition, 1960, 238, x.

and/or narcissism. The leading exponents of that position are Thomas Hobbes and Bernard de Mandeville.

Of these, Hobbes is better known by far, but only because his work was more ambitious in its scope. His recent champions, like Michael Oakeshott and John Gray, have revised his old reputation as an apologist for despotism. But not even they can seriously deny that he had a dismal view of existence.[13] True, Hobbes implies that mental and spiritual improvement might be possible for those who leave the anarchic state of nature; one of the drawbacks of that condition is that there can be 'no knowledge of the face of the earth; no account of time; no arts; no letters; no society.' Yet his view of our innate characteristics 'hollows out' all of these activities; we only accumulate wisdom, or mingle with each other, in order to satisfy our 'perpetual and restless desire for power after power, that ceaseth only in death.' In other words, human beings are so constructed that nothing but power can ever be acquired for its own sake. If a strong government removes 'continual fear, and danger of violent death', life need not be 'poor' or 'short'; but even in civil society it can hardly be anything but 'solitary', 'nasty' and 'brutish' unless we change the accepted meaning of these words (something that Hobbes was predictably keen to do).[14]

De Mandeville had a similar view of human beings, and he breaks the bad news with Hobbesian relish. In *The Fable of the Bees* (1705) he argued that the traits that are normally condemned as vices are really good for business, and that economic progress would halt if people embraced morality and stopped trying to outshine their neighbours. On this view even thieves are indirect benefactors of mankind, particularly if they steal from people who hoard up money rather than spending it. De Mandeville argued that morality is spurious anyway, since we only ever act to gratify ourselves. He was also bold enough to admit that a liberal economic order depends on the active denial

[13] See Ian Tregenza, *Michael Oakeshott on Hobbes: A study in the renewal of philosophical ideas*, Imprint Academic, 2003, and John Gray, 'Hobbes and the modern state', in *Post-Liberalism: Studies in Political Thought*, Routledge, 1996.

[14] Thomas Hobbes, *Leviathan*, Blackwell edition, no date, 82 [+ 2nd ref].

of real opportunities to 'a multitude of the Laborious Poor', whose knowledge 'should be confin'd within the Verge of their Occupations' to prevent them from imagining any alternative to their drudgery.[15]

They might be outnumbered among the great names of Western political theory, but Hobbes and de Mandeville sound much more in tune with contemporary experience than the 'fleshed-out' liberals like Mill or Milton. We might consider that liberty is worth having because it offers the possibility of self-development; but nowadays we have good reason to think that this opportunity will remain theoretical. On the other hand, it is very easy to associate liberty with the chance of material acquisition — to equate 'progress' with the accumulation of consumer goods, regardless of the methods employed. Even the late John Rawls, who hoped to salvage something from the old liberal tradition, could only do so by positing a surreal scenario in which individuals construct a theory of justice behind a 'veil of ignorance' that precludes any knowledge of their personal circumstances, abilities or aspirations.[16] We might be better off than de Mandeville's 'Laborious Poor' in certain respects; but increasingly our worthwhile knowledge is 'confin'd within the Verge of our Occupations'. We live, in short, in a time when hollowed-out liberalism dominates the itinerary; the fleshy version is in danger of becoming a mere curiosity in the lumber-room of literature.

Some might conclude that fleshed-out liberal theory placed excessive demands on human nature, presupposing a future state of perfection rather than a tolerable existence. That was the kind of thinking that gave some credence to Berlin's strictures against 'positive' liberty. Generally speaking, liberal 'perfectionists' tended to argue that the state should take responsibility for bringing about their goal (although one of their number, William Godwin, went to the opposite extreme and recommended that the state should be abolished). But even if Berlin is right in warning against the perfectionists, his argument has far less

[15] Bernard de Mandeville, *The Fable of the Bees*, Pelican edition, 1970, 294.
[16] John Rawls, *A Theory of Justice*, Oxford University Press edition, 1972.

weight against those who set their sights a bit lower — to something like Aristotle's 'Golden Mean'. After all, many people have tried to become a little wiser, and a little kinder, in the course of their lives; and some of them have succeeded. Yet people do not live in the abstract; and in today's context anyone who tries to work towards this goal is thinking and behaving as if the twentieth century never happened. This is not the place to explore the reasons for the triumph of hollowed-out liberalism, although Total War and technological change would have a prominent place in any explanation. But we should at least note one intellectual trend, which is clearly associated with these developments.

It might be supposed that postmodernism could have no bearing on disputes among liberals. After all, it questions everything (except itself); and having concluded that there are no rational answers, it celebrates diversity. That seems pretty harmless: even laudable. But 'diversity' today can only be one-dimensional, when all but our most outlandish non-conformists are affiliated to the hollow branch of the liberal family.[17] In practice the postmodern attack on rationality falls heavily on fleshed-out liberalism and leaves the hollowed-out version untouched. Even moderately fleshed-out liberalism sets a stiffer task for the concept of reason; that is why Katie is right to say that her beliefs are 'complicated, and tiring'. In particular, it urges that people should look beyond what appears to be their immediate interest. Now, hollowed-out liberalism is the philosophy of the short term, of the speed-dating, cold-calling society. Postmodernism might teach that this kind of life is no more (or less) 'rational' than an existence based on respect for others. But those who feel at home in our times only use the word 'reason' out of linguistic laziness. When they say that their way of life is 'rational' they really mean that it is a lot of fun. For them reason

---

[17] Bruce Charlton and Peter Andras argue that 'the persistence and increase of modern pluralism suggests that it cannot be unacceptable for most people most of the time', so we should not lose sleep over the decline of 'moral coherence'. A few pages later we find them welcoming the erosion of genuine cultural differences in the developed world, and advocating 'pharmacological interventions, or genetic modifications of humans', to overcome the absence of any real spiritual satisfaction in modern life (*The Modernization Imperative*, Imprint Academic, 2003, 42, 61).

does not even play the secondary role allotted to it by David Hume. Once their passions have told them what they want, they do not stop to work out the most sensible way of getting it; they just make a grab.[18]

It is probably no coincidence that the academic vogue for postmodernism arose at roughly the same time as the craze for 'political correctness' — an attempt to shift the attack on intolerance from attitudes to words, from realities to symbols.[19] Even at its best-intentioned, political correctness seems ominously hollow, encouraging people to confuse a sanitised vocabulary with an increase in enlightenment. It might have persuaded some people, on certain issues, to re-examine a few of their unreflective presuppositions. But at its worst, it endangers even our current one-dimensional shadow of pluralistic discussion. The typical tactic of the politically correct is to proceed by dictat, circumventing the open debate favoured by the old liberals, and lapsing into a kind of terminological totalitarianism.

Political correctness has infuriated hollowed-out liberals in Britain and the United States. But they have no need to worry. We might be trying harder to avoid articulating our prejudices against particular groups, but our respect for each other as human beings has been declining much faster. Indeed, political correctness could never have emerged in its present form if we *had* retained that respect. Anyone who thinks that a compulsory course in tolerance-training can overcome decades of exposure to anti-social attitudes must have a pretty condescending view of human nature.

---

[18] Or, as Keiron O'Hara observes, the Classical distinction between 'reason' and 'appetite' is no longer recognised; see *Trust: From Socrates to Spin*, Icon Books, 2004, 211.

[19] As Simon Barnes recently reflected during the furore over racist comments by the football pundit Ron Atkinson, 'It seems that the appearance of racism is worse than racism itself'; *Times*, 23 April 2004. This was certainly a case of words being louder than action, because when he was a prominent manager Atkinson had been one of the first to foster the careers of several gifted black players. He was punished for his infelicitous expressions at a time when premiership teams still included a number of people who had been connected inconclusively with off-the-field violence and sexual assaults.

We can best understand political correctness as a sign that fleshed-out liberals have capitulated. For many years they have been living a contradiction of their own. Their philosophy makes them hope for the best, but their circumstances force them to fear the worst. If the prospect of defeat were not bad enough in itself, they have their noses rubbed in it every day. Hollowed-out liberalism is everywhere. In the House of Commons, it sneers at itself across the dispatch boxes; in the law courts it sues itself for compensation; and it fills acres of newsprint with its soul-sapping tales of celebrity and conspicuous consumption. Yet although we have lost the rounded vision of human progress without which the great liberal thinkers would never have reached for their ink-pots and quills, the beneficiaries of their defeat are justifying themselves by uttering slogans derived from their work without acknowledgement.

The original arguments in favour of universal suffrage and a free press were advanced on premises which have not yet been entirely disproved. But it is unsettling to recall that, not so very long ago, people advocated votes for all adults on the naïve assumption that this would ensure good government, with the added bonus that the exercise of the franchise would promote a rational and responsible electorate. The original case for freedom of speech has fared no better. If by some medical miracle Milton were still living at this hour, and heard his passionate defence of the printed word being used to justify the contents of today's tabloids, his only consolation would be his inability to read them.

Whether or not fleshed-out liberalism is good for anything but opposition is an interesting question, on which the jury is still deliberating. It would only be just, though, for its remaining modern representatives to rise up and reclaim the slogans that rightfully belong to them. The problem is that while the political theorists of the past tried to change the world in their different ways, today's preconceptions seem impregnable to argument. That hollowed-out Hegelian, Francis Fukuyama, claims that liberal democracy must be preferable to its predecessors because although many civilisations have lavished praise on themselves, our own age is more 'reflective'. The extent of that reflective capability was revealed after the murderous attack on the World Trade Center. The overwhelming majority of Fukuyama's compatriots quickly concluded that it was a direct assault against democratic values. This might have been *partly* true, but no 'reflective' society could have accepted it as the whole explanation. It provided a convenient cue for self-congratulation, rather than provoking any serious soul-searching.

In Britain the reaction to 9/11 was much more nuanced. But then again, the attack did not take place within the UK. If that had been the case, the likely response can be judged from the most recent precedent of a traumatic episode – the death of Princess Diana. This also ended up as an excuse for the public to flatter itself, through the medium of Tony Blair's gut-wrenching tribute to 'The People's Princess'. The fact that members of the public had been directly responsible for the death by spurring on the paparazzi could be forgotten. With no liberal catch-phrases to protect them, the monarchy provided an ideal alternative for the scapegoat-hunting press and public.

The success of liberalism in the West has owed much to this ability to provide a collective ego-boost. Bernard de Mandeville thought that flattery was 'the most powerful Argument that cou'd be used to human creatures'[20]. But one does not have to endorse the Hobbesian view of humanity to accept that people like being told that they are already rational enough to enjoy freedom, and to expect that they will react with intense hostility if someone tries to tell them otherwise. Fleshed-out individuals might pause to judge whether praise is justified; but even they will be biased in favour of the flatterer. The hollowed-out will never hesitate; even in the mouth of an exposed hypocrite, unearned praise will please them more than the cautions of a plain speaker. Thus the essential qualification for freedom – the hard-earned prize of self-knowledge – will always be claimed prematurely by the ignorant, and denied for longest by those who are fit to be free. The inevitable result is a passive assemblage of consumer-subjects rather than a body of citizens, and a state which pampers and punishes with no positive purpose.

---

[20]   De Mandeville, *Fable of the Bees*, 82.

A lot of ground has been covered here, so a brief recap is in order. I have argued that liberalism can be divided into two camps: 'fleshed-out' and 'hollowed-out'. These categories bear more relevance to the modern condition than Berlin's distinction between negative and positive liberty, because the ultimate pre-occupation of all liberals lies with the individual rather than the state. Fleshed-out liberals believe that material acquisition is at best a means to an end; hollowed-out liberals think that it is everything. The overwhelming majority of writers in the liberal tradition have belonged to the 'fleshed-out' school; without a vision of human improvement they would never have written a word. For a variety of reasons, slogans derived from their writings have proved irresistible. But the substance has long departed; not, in my own view, because all of those fleshed-out liberal thinkers were wildly optimistic in their demands upon the capacity of human beings, but because they were flattering enough to lure significant numbers of people to endorse their ideas before they were properly equipped to do so.

On this view, liberalism turns out to be a lot like Marxism — a commendable idea, put into practice by very flawed people and grievously distorted by the practitioners. Surely there can be no comparable danger in the victory of liberalism, whether premature or not? Probably fewer crimes have been committed in its name. John Gray has pointed out the underlying similarities between Western regimes and Al Qaeda: all are distinctive products of modernity.[21] One might quibble that, for the most part, the casualties of the West are collateral. But the hollowed-out liberal regimes of Bush and Blair have killed thousands of people in Iraq without noticeable regret.[22] And the 'thinking' that inspired the conflict epitomises the hollowed-out liberal mindset. The anonymous victims were pulverised by high-level bombing because they deserved a better life. The survivors were meant to

---

[21] John Gray, *Al Qaeda And What It Means To Be Modern*, Faber and Faber (2003).

[22] As this section was being revised some American and British soldiers were implicated in the ill-treatment of Iraqi detainees, apparently acting on the same sadistic impulses which had inspired Saddam Hussein's functionaries.

act in accordance with the meanest possible interpretation even of short-term rationality; suitably impressed by an exposure to 'shock and awe', they were expected to rush out and embrace their attackers. There was no reason at all for confidence that a Saddam-free country would embrace Western liberalism under any circumstances. But US policy-makers apparently assumed that the 'liberation' would turn all Iraqis into card-carrying members of the Republican Party. If they did not accept the Western outlook all at once, they were sure to do so once they had been exposed to a free press, and exercised the right to vote. While they were discovering their true consumerist selves, Iraqis could be treated like vermin by the occupying forces. In a piece of Orwellian word-play, anyone who resisted for whatever reason could be branded as an 'insurgent'. According to the visions of the ludicrously-misnamed American 'neo-conservatives', once the liberalisation was complete the rest of the Middle East would follow suit — with the exception of the Israelis, who are reckoned to be Republicans already. These arguments were doubly de-contextualised; even in the West they had tacitly been abandoned along with the fleshed-out idea of progress. But hollowed-out liberals deployed them to conceal their lust for profit. Unfortunately, some fleshed-out liberals allowed themselves to be persuaded into seconding their efforts, so great is the naivety of their lust for human improvement.

Once any set of ideas is ripped from its original context, some kind of trouble can be expected. In the hollowed-out form which traduces the memory of its founding fathers, Western liberalism has turned out to be a snake which disembowels its victims before consuming them. But is hollowed-out liberalism the signature tune for the 'end of history'? The nature of this beast — its misleading and alluring simplicity — suggests a different outcome. For the liberal snake has been cursed with a Hobbesian appetite. Its rejection of anything more elevated than short-term 'rationality', and the absence of other food supplies, leaves it with only one option. It has started to feast on itself.

Chapter 2

The Media

If the media mislead, or if readers cannot assess their reporting, the wells of public discourse are poisoned — Onora O'Neill[1]

If contemporary British liberalism is a snake with a hyperactive appetite, the tabloid press must be the fangs which inject a paralysing poison. But surely it would be wrong to throw the blanket term of liberalism across the whole of our media? Does it make any sense, for example, to describe the prevailing values of our tabloids as 'liberal'? There is no room here to do more than appeal to the preceding argument as evidence that the tabloids are in fact the very epitome of contemporary, hollowed-out liberalism. Whatever parties they choose to support, they stand for the full set of ideas listed above. And like liberalism, they owe their success to a mixture of flattery and contempt.

Broad-brush condemnations of the media usually provoke protests on behalf of the honourable exceptions: remaining investigative journalists committed to the search for truth; columnists on the op-ed pages who retain some affection for the English language; broadcasters who lust after quality rather than ratings; satirists who stigmatise corruption and hypocrisy wherever it lurks. We could spend many pages on the nature and causes of the BBC's weaknesses, but we would also have to acknowledge its surviving strengths. Amongst our newspapers, the broadsheets are generally hailed as the final refuge of rectitude. The very inconvenience of the format is seen as a guarantee of intellectual and moral resilience — hence the heart-burnings

[1]   A Question of Trust, Cambridge University Press, 2002, 90.

when some of these papers recently decided to produce tabloid editions.

No-one can deny that there is a difference. There is more solid sense and pleasing prose even on the sports pages of one day's *Guardian* than the combined wit or wisdom in a year of the tabloids. Sometimes it seems as if the staff of British newspapers have been sending despatches from two distinct countries, united only by a common name and the same TV listings. There was an excellent example at the end of June 2004, when the *Times* and the *Sun* reflected on the hurried 'handover of power' to a nominated government in Iraq. In the first, the headline of Simon Jenkins' piece was 'They promised to stay until the job was done. Instead, they have cut and run'. The headline itself contained more accurate information than the whole of the front-page *Sun* report, which ran under the euphoric banner of 'Job Done'. Even Rupert Murdoch, the proprietor of both newspapers, might have lost his usual sense of certainty if he saw their conflicting coverage.[2]

But are these publications different *in kind*, or just markedly different in degree? Is the same crooked worm which infests the tabloids also at work within the broadsheets?

There are good grounds for supposing that this is the case. John Stuart Mill believed that truth will always overcome falsehood, if each is given a fair trial. He envisaged a fairly protracted contest between rival publications much like his beloved *Westminster Review* — finding friendly fault with each others' arguments, but never doubting that the dispute was rooted in sincere principle and backed up by indigestible statistics. Mill was safely in his grave before the emergence of press barons, for whom questions of truth or falsehood were trumped by the quest for profit. But even if his worst nightmare had come true in his lifetime Mill would have expected the spite, hypocrisy and joyless exploitation enshrined in tabloid newspapers to be overthrown by the voices of reason — not immediately, perhaps, but certainly within one hundred and fifty years of the publication of *On Liberty*.

---

[2]   See the *Times* and the *Sun* of 30 June 2004.

There is, of course, a broadsheet battle of a kind. But it is not really about the cause of truth. It is mostly about numbers (hence the new 'tabloid' broadsheets). And it is a circulation war within an isolated limb of the body politic. One can rejoice that the overall market share of the *Times*, *Telegraph*, *Guardian* and *Independent* has remained fairly constant over recent years. But it is constantly small; and every downward fluctuation evokes a fear of a developing trend. Nearly two hundred years ago, William Hazlitt thought that the *Times* was 'pompous, dogmatical, and full of pretentions. ... It takes up no failing cause; fights no uphill battle; advocates no great principle; holds out a helping hand to no oppressed or obscure individual'.[3] All this might still be true today. But even those who disagree with the general editorial line of the *Times*, and deplore the influence of its proprietor, would feel some regret at the suppression of the newspaper itself. Its disappearance would leave another hole in the defensive wall of civilised society.

Yet we should not rest content with the mere survival of time-honoured titles. There would be no cause for celebration if the broadsheets were retaining their readers but losing their essence — if they are being hollowed out by tabloid values. A quick glance at an average issue is enough to show how far this process has gone. Fastidious observers might bemoan the tendency to present commentary as fact, but in today's context this is a trivial, contestable point. The real trouble lies elsewhere. Some of the surveys published by the broadsheets provide useful raw material to inform an overall picture of the strange British blend of hedonism and dejection. But whole pages are filled with snapshots of transient tastes, in films, pop music and even classic novels or historical heroes. Attentive broadsheet readers have no fear of losing touch with the latest 'celebrity' gossip.[4] Typi-

---

[3]   William Hazlitt, 'The Periodical Press', in *Contributions to the Edinburgh Review*, Vol. XVI, *Complete Works*, Dent & Sons, 1933, 225.

[4]   The Times of 19 April 2004 featured a page-length colour photograph of Prince William in swimming-trunks. Much of the attached article was taken up with speculation about the fashionable status of the trunks. The strapline on the page reminded the reader that the paper considered this item to be 'news'.

cally, this information is supplied with a knowing wink to the reader, as if to say 'Of course, we're all too wise and grown-up to take any of this stuff seriously'. But the danger does not lie in the unlikely possibility of readers taking it seriously. We should not have to take it at all, in any state of mind.

The problem, in part, is one of complacency. Our tabloids are now so deplorable that the broadsheets have lost any incentive to excel. Broadsheet sales might be endangered by the emergence of new media like the internet, and politicians may treat them with disdain instead of fearing their investigative prowess. But even if they are only half-right, the broadsheets can remain wholly self-righteous so long as they are *not the tabloids*. They are in danger of falling into a trap prepared by their critics, providing fare which would only be adequate for a hollow elite, clinging to an empty eminence after giving up any hope of proselytising on behalf of genuine cultural achievement. At the same time, as the old editorial hands drift away from the media they are being replaced by a new generation which has been taught to respect the popular appeal of the tabloids — and even to admire the cynicism of their best-known columnists. Whatever they might have achieved in a different era, we can hardly depend upon the judgement of people who have been too much in the *Sun*. Their highest ambition is to furnish material for 'water-cooler' conversations among high-spending professionals — the favoured victims of the ratings-warriors and the advertising pimps — who are taught to think that a sense of workplace community can be faked through the brisk exchange of banal opinions about fashion, film or celebrity scandal.

The danger is not that the broadsheets will sink into exact duplicates of the tabloid outlook at any given time. The process of 'dumbing down' must have some limit, and it is unlikely that the broadsheets of the future will ever be as grim as the tabloids of today. Even so, the initiative in terms of style and content has been with the tabloids for so long that one can only expect a continuation of an unmistakable levelling tendency of tone — not least because semi-ironic coverage of tabloid stories and spurious surveys provides cheap copy for the broadsheets. Thus lists of the rich and the famous, which might have provided a regular continuation of Anthony Sampson's pioneering 'Anatomies of Britain', are now presented as nothing more than pecuniary pornography for the aspiring and the envious. The Hobbesian materialism which provides a hallmark to the hollow has even intruded into the *Guardian*, where one might have expected prolonged and ferocious resistance. One of its star columnists, Jonathan Freedland, has written that 'Once we are satisfied that everyone taking part has an equal shot at the top — as they do in the lottery — then we can tolerate the widest inequalities, as they do in America.'[5] Not 'an equal chance of a worthwhile life'; 'an equal shot at the top'. So much for John Rawls, and the praiseworthy ideals which emerge from behind his 'veil of ignorance'! There is no longer any talk in the mainstream media of justifying inequalities only insofar as they benefit the worst off in society. Even the bogus argument about a 'trickle-down effect' seems to have been stopped at source. We can have no room for such milk-and-water liberalism in our bracing, leap-frogging society where cut-throat competition will be allowed to cease only with death — so long as, according to some arbitrary criteria, we are satisfied that everyone has had an 'equal shot' before they drop.

Thus, although apologists for liberalism can still boast of diversity in the British media, these variations are essentially superficial in scope and depth. The broadsheet press and analytical television programmes like *Channel 4 News* or *Newsnight* are incapable of supplying an effective antidote to the tabloid poison.

So what are tabloid values? It goes without saying that they provide superficial coverage and simplistic moral judgements on complex issues. This cannot really count as an offence; it is merely part of the tabloid job-description. But even if the format lends itself to superficiality and over-simplification, there is no need for them to indulge in deliberate distortion. If a charge of 'institutionalised hypocrisy' is unduly provocative, one might say instead that they are 'insufficiently motivated to avoid contradictory utterances'. Within a single issue of the same newspa-

---

[5]   *Bring Home the Revolution*, 244.

per we often stumble across conflicting messages, usually in the field of sexual morality. Conduct which is praised in one context is blasted in another. The gossip columnists invite us to envy a decadent lifestyle, while the agony aunts order us to avoid it. Moving from morality to the world of finance, we find advertisements for exorbitant loans jostling with sombre warnings about the nightmare of indebtedness. But the phenomenon is seen at its best over the medium term, and by readers who subscribe to more than one tabloid. The fortunes of individual 'celebrities' will be decided not by their activities, but by their attitude towards the respective publications. The offer of exclusive access is a guarantee of sympathy from one paper, and unrelenting hostility in another. If the celebrity switches allegiance, the nature of the coverage undergoes a similar transformation; a male 'hunk' will now become a 'love-rat', and a 'curvy' female 'stunna' will be crucified for her cellulite.[6] Nothing could be easier for the people who compose such articles; from the outset, the relationship on both sides is an unstable mixture of gratitude and contempt, so a simple instruction will be quite sufficient to dictate the tone of a particular piece.

The same process is at work in the section of the tabloids which is devoted to issues of public concern, like the state of the housing market. This is a tabloid favourite, for understandable reasons. Hollowed-out liberals can only approve of the madness which has made us regard our dwelling-places as so many chips in a casino. Property prices may go up or down; a paper fortune can turn overnight into a summons to the bankruptcy court. But the tabloids will always be there, trying to be the first to cheer a boom or jeer at the victims of a slump. What they will never do, of course, is to explain this quintessentially British phenomenon. Demand exceeds supply not just because of our lust for acquisition and profit. Family life increasingly resembles Hobbes's state of nature, and the only answer is for every adult to occupy a separate house. Meanwhile the electronic media churns out

---

[6] On rare occasions, the ratings war has the salutary effect of enforcing deviations into tolerable tabloid behaviour. Recently The *Sun* dropped a scoffing headline about a troubled 'celebrity' when its first edition had provoked protests from 'readers'.

endless 'makeover' programmes, offering tips on how to beautify the backdrop to an ugly life. The process becomes self-perpetuating, as couples who might otherwise be happy together are torn apart by financial worries. Even those who stay together will be damaged in some way, as they join forces with estate agents to lie about their 'deceptively spacious' properties and plot to secure a place within the catchment area of the best schools.

The housing market is a notable feature of the second tabloid trait: the assumption of a minimal attention-span among readers. The favourite organs of Middle England, the *Mail* and the *Express*, are particularly keen to predict the collapse of property prices. They will produce a blood-curdling front-page splash on the subject, as soon as they think their readers have forgotten the previous one. But scare stories are particularly vulnerable to the law of dwindling returns, and their longevity in the headlines bears only a distant relationship to their foundation in fact. They will last a little longer if hatred can be mixed with the fear. Newspapers will stick to an issue is there is a chance of blaming a vulnerable social group for a problem, or forcing the government into over-hasty or unnecessary action. Thus some tabloids thundered on remorselessly about the combined vaccine for measles, mumps and rubella (MMR), because the government decided to back up the view of medical experts. The froth had barely been wiped away when the *Times* reported (on page 9) that cases of the 'superbug' MRSA 'have risen more than 15-fold over the past decade' — that is, roughly since the tabloids grew tired of running stories about bacteria-resistant diseases.[7]

The third tabloid tendency can only be called brazen affrontery. If a body like the General Medical Council (GMC) governed the activities of tabloid journalists, a sizeable proportion would be debarred from practising every year. Yet in the tabloid trade, mistakes which would condemn a professional in any other sphere are condoned — even rewarded — provided that they do not suppress sales (or, in the case of Andrew Gilligan, infuriate the government's chief spin doctor). In the

gossip pages, ancient tittle-tattle is related as if it had happened
yesterday; in the recent furore over the cultural views of Robert
Kilroy-Silk, we learned that lengthy articles can be recycled, and
the ensuing complaints will concern the content rather than the
repetition. Yet from this subterranean vantage point, the tabloids think that they have a free licence to snipe at public servants, even those who have made excusable mistakes after a
long and blameless career.

We are beginning to slide into the endlessly-regressive argument about whether or not the public gets the newspapers it
deserves. While honest disagreement on this subject is possible,
one can certainly say that if we do deserve our tabloids we must
have offended very badly to merit so little. The brilliant barrister
Geoffrey Robertson believes that the worst of our newspapers
'mirror rather than create the national character'.[8] This verdict is
difficult to square with one of those opinion polls which actually
conveys important information, in this case showing that only
15 per cent of Britons trust the newspapers they read.[9] To reinforce the point, in most popularity polls journalists end up near
the bottom, even losing out to politicians.

Of course, people who look in the mirror often dislike their
own reflections, and it is easier to blame a mirror than to alter
one's appearance. Yet it is strange that an industry which places
so much emphasis on expressions of public opinion should have
passed over these particular findings so easily. They are, after
all, fairly shocking results. Even though more than two centuries
have passed since the Enlightenment, it would be unreasonable
to expect the average Briton to have developed the wit and erudition of a Voltaire. But it should not be utopian to hope that the
public might have come to share something of the sturdy judgement of Voltaire's valet, and choose a daily paper accordingly.
On Robertson's view, the British public fails this test. It might
realise that the press is trivial and untrustworthy, but it lacks the
self-knowledge to realise that in blaming the mirror it is pro-

[8]   Geoffrey Robertson, *The Justice Game*, Vintage, 1999, 350.
[9]   See the entry on 'National Daily Newspapers', in Mark Garnett and
      Richard Weight, *Modern British History: The Essential Guide*, Pimlico
      edition, 2004.

claiming its own stupidity. In this respect, at least, we seem to be relaxed inhabitants of postmodernity.

There is, fortunately, a more optimistic interpretation: that the public knows how bad the papers are, but lacks the power to set up a more accurate mirror because of the perverse operations of the free market in information. It's also possible to suggest a compromise between these positions. Even at their worst, the tabloids do seem to reflect an unfortunate element of the British 'national character' — 'prurience' is the most accurate word (and seems only to be used in this context, like 'beleaguered' in relation to troubled football managers). Yet at worst the British public is *selectively* prurient, while tabloid prurience is indiscriminate and unrelenting. On this view, the question of trust is barely relevant to tabloid fortunes. Most people regard them as a branch of the entertainment industry. When they hit congenial targets, they are sufficiently amusing to compensate for weeks of malevolent misfiring. But even when we enjoy their exploits — when a minor celebrity is 'shamed', or we discover that the Queen allows tupperware on her breakfast table — we are laughing at the victims, not applauding the assailants. We trust ourselves not to trust them.

If this is right, we should still consider whether we are paying too high a price for our entertainment. Given the kind of hollowed-out, impoverished standard of 'reason' which has crept in across the range of our activities, it would not be surprising if we had seen through the superficial tricks of the tabloid press while being comprehensively bamboozled at a deeper level. In the nature of things, unconscious influence is very difficult to identify. But we would be foolishly complacent to assume that our general view of the world can emerge unscathed even from a second-hand encounter with the tabloid press. In a society where uncontrived contact with others is increasingly rare, we have every reason to suppose that the people in our unavoidable encounters are very much like the hollowed-out characters we are constantly reading about, either in the tabloids themselves or in the parasitic broadsheets. They teach us that people are either means to our own ends, or obstacles to our enjoyment. So we spend most of our lives like our supermarket selves, elbowing and jostling our way through throngs of strangers. If Immanuel Kant had ever seen a check-out queue, he would never have come up with his Categorical Imperative.

But we must beware of repeating Berlin's mistake, and attributing too much influence to the printed or spoken word. True to form, the tabloids themselves are inconsistent on this question. When their favoured party wins a general election, or a minister capitulates to public pressure, they are quick to claim responsibility. When things turn out contrary to their wishes — when, for example, they unleash vigilante gangs against innocent people — they fall silent. Probably even hardened tabloid hacks venture out every morning with a residual hope that their activities will create some difference (if not improvement) in the world. So whatever they thought of the election result celebrated in the headline 'It's the *Sun* Wot Won It!', they must endorse the general principle behind it. Yet at a more general level they would probably agree with Geoffrey Robertson in thinking that they merely *reflect* the existing attitudes of the British public. They are only there to serve, etc., etc..

The precise influence of The *Sun* over the result of the 1992 general election is warmly disputed.[10] Quite possibly, its depiction of Neil Kinnock as a light bulb, which voters were invited to switch off before leaving the country, only reinforced existing attitudes to that unfortunate politician. Yet whether or not it affected the result, many people were prepared to accept its claims at face value. Public opinion is a hall of mirrors, where a reputation for influence is influence in itself. In any case, more profound evidence of the tabloid effect could be found elsewhere. After that election, opinion pollsters began to refer to a 'spiral of silence' — a refusal of citizens to express their genuine views when they were canvassed. It was assumed that some voters were too ashamed to admit that they intended to vote Conservative; so in future a coefficient of hypocrisy had to be built

---

[10] See, for example, Kenneth Newton, 'Caring and Competence: The Long, Long Campaign', in Anthony King et al, *Britain at the Polls 1992*, Chatham House, 1992, 156-59.

into opinion poll findings. Labour's response was to nullify the spiral of silence by adopting the presumed preferences of all the people who had lied before the election. In short, its leaders decided that the electorate really had been moulded by tabloid values of hypocrisy, affrontery and boredom. They pitched their 'big tent' accordingly. Before the 1997 election they surrendered to the *Sun*, which was about to abandon the Conservatives anyway.

It is typical of this convoluted tale that the politician who showed the greatest defiance — and ended up running headlong into the fangs of the snake — was a member of the party which really did owe something to the support of the tabloids. In December 1989 David Mellor, Mrs Thatcher's minister for national heritage, warned that the popular press was 'drinking in the last chance saloon'. Although the press had already been the subject of three futile Royal Commissions (1947–9, 61–2, 74–7), Britain's elected politicians still felt unable to deal directly with the Fourth Estate. A Home Office committee was established under David Calcutt, the Master of Magdalene College Cambridge. In June 1990 this body recommended a tough privacy law. But despite public support the government was still reluctant to take on the tabloids. As a compromise, the industry's impotent regulator, the Press Council, disappeared. It was replaced by a Press Complaints Commission (PCC).

If John Stuart Mill had been around to ensure that Mellor's arguments had a fair hearing, the tabloids might have been tamed. Instead, his weak-willed successors lined up to throw a protective blanket of liberal principle over people whose idea of 'freedom' stretched no further than the range of a telephoto lens. The PCC could never be anything more than another toothless tortoise. Its potency can be gauged from the fact that the notorious 1992 campaign was its first electoral test. It was, of course, Mellor himself whose drinking was almost done. His career was shredded by the tabloids less than six months after that election.

We are supposed to take comfort from the fact that the industry's representatives on the PCC are now outnumbered by lay people, who can be presumed to know what Mill really meant when he defended the liberty of the press. Yet the composition of the PCC is irrelevant. Its purpose is to polish the fangs, not to rip them out. Some individuals have gained token redress from glaring examples of intrusion; and the PCC has encouraged ordinary citizens to complain on these grounds, reaching beyond the ubiquitous celebrities whose courtship of publicity undermines the whole exercise. But editors and proprietors knew in advance that the real problem would never be tackled. The PCC's code of practice (1990) stated that 'Newspapers and periodicals should take care not to publish inaccurate, misleading or distorted material'. This clause was retained in the revised version of 1999.[11] There might be limited scope for argument about 'inaccurate' reporting, but 'misleading' and 'distorted' are in the eye of the beholder. On any reasonable definition, they are in the eyes of every tabloid reader on a daily basis; it is, after all, their business to purvey a 'misleading' and 'distorted' view of human existence. Yet a rigorous implementation of these terms by the PCC would lead to an all-out confrontation between the regulator and the organs of widest circulation. This would be an unequal contest in a liberal society. The PCC is appointed, whereas the tabloids have been tossed a democratic mandate from the millions who either buy and disbelieve, or look at the pictures before throwing the paper in the dustbin.

Ideally, the PCC should be able to compel some newspapers to print the words 'This publication is likely to contain grave distortions, and will contradict itself on consecutive pages' — or, more crisply, 'For heaven's sake don't take any of this seriously' — in large, vivid letters on their front pages. Sadly, the current vogue for protecting the public against itself is most unlikely to extend so far. Thanks to the PCC, we can be confident that the hounding of celebrities will be punished with slaps on the wrist after the damage has been done, and steps have been taken to ensure that convicted criminals do not benefit from selling their stories. But these are cosmetic exercises. The real problem is the general presentation of human nature in the tabloid

[11]   See Richard Shannon, *A Press Free and Responsible: Self-regulation and the Press Complaints Commission 1991-2001*, John Murray, 2001.

pages, and the PCC is powerless to act against this. At least its activities are not counter-productive, which is the sorry fate of the Advertising Standards Authority (ASA). Set up in 1961, the ASA invigilates the most hollow of all Western 'industries', struggling to ensure that its products are 'legal, decent, honest and truthful'. In practice, it has to define these terms in a way which suits the very people it is supposed to be policing. Its code asserts bravely that 'Adverse publicity is damaging to most marketers and serves to warn the public.' In a fleshed-out society this would be true; but then there would be no need for the ASA, because rational individuals would simply boycott any product which depended on 'indecent' or 'dishonest' advertising, without the intervention of any outside agency. As it is, companies can be fairly sure that a campaign which falls foul of the Authority will secure additional free publicity from the media, and that those who take offence will be outnumbered by potential customers who are amused by the fuss.[12]

There are, though, some good reasons to think that change is on its way. We have claimed that the liberal snake is consuming itself; and the first effects are likely to be registered in the media. We can already appreciate the extent to which the 'free press' is undermining the key liberal idea of an impartial judicial system. Several tabloids have been chastised for causing the collapse of trials because of prejudicial reporting. Believing that they are above the law, it is only natural for them to think that they are entitled to manipulate the way in which it affects lesser mortals. There is still an understandable reluctance to jail editors for contempt of court; but repeated offences might be bringing the day closer. Meanwhile, the media is bringing itself into contempt through its treatment of particular offenders. For example, the tabloids devoted acres of newsprint to alleged parallels between

[12] In 2003 the ASA received a record number of complaints for a single advertisement. In a campaign designed to draw attention to the problem of child poverty, the charity Barnados used several controversial images, including a baby with a cockroach crawling out of its mouth. The protests of a mere 475 people made it the most widely-discussed advertisement of the year — even more so than the government's £4 million campaign to delude people into thinking that clogged arteries are invariably the result of cigarette smoking.

Maxine Carr and the late Myra Hindley. Their cases were indeed comparable: both were women who received disproportionate blame from the media for hideous crimes in which a male was the prime mover. Carr had not even been present, but somehow the tabloids managed to imply that this made her more guilty than the actual culprit. She committed perjury because of her misplaced love for a man; and this laid her open to continual harassment from newspapers who commit contempt of court for the love of profit. If they could not prevent Carr's release, the tabloids could ruin her rehabilitation. When a court order prevented them from revealing details of her new life, several editors rushed to appeal on the grounds that this infringed the sacred freedom of speech. Finally, in July 2004 there was an attempt to expose Carr's supposedly pampered existence in the public interest, which only resulted in court action to tighten the legal cordon around her privacy.

This sorry kind of stuff might have worked in the days when Henry VIII executed a wife for failing to produce a male heir, or when women were burned alive for being eccentric. Over six centuries the attitudes which informed these atrocities have been somewhat discredited, despite the efforts of 'post-feminists'. The only people who seem to have missed these intellectual developments are tabloid editors. But their contempt for human beings is not confined to females. They feel much the same about celebrities. Now, that might seem odd because these are the people whose activities provide the tabloids with most of their 'news'. But celebrities nowadays are disposable commodities, and newspapers have learned that they can be manufactured out of the most unpromising materials. This is convenient, because people who rise to public attention through genuine abilities are less likely to pander to the market for demeaning 'exclusives'. They simply don't need to do so. People who want privacy are, frankly, boring; far better to focus on hollowed-out individuals whose lives would implode in the absence of a camera.

We should never forget that celebrity is the hollow half-sister of fame, and any kind of 'celebrity culture' is a form of secular religion which underlines our inadequacies.[13] Even so, there has undoubtedly been a change in recent years, which is clearly related to our contemporary predicament. We argued above that liberalism requires something like equal respect for other individuals, and that although we still satisfy that criterion we are coming to regard others with roughly equal contempt. It is easy to exaggerate the extent to which celebrities used to be admired, rather than envied. But admiration certainly was part of the mix. Nowadays, even celebrities who are held up as 'role models' by the press are under perpetual scrutiny for evidence of personal frailties. In most cases the media builds up individuals purely for the purpose of tearing them down. From the media perspective, these are victimless crimes. Everyone involved in the game knows the rules and acknowledges the forfeit for anyone who is left with a losing hand. If only it were so simple. Gradually we are learning to feel contempt even for the people who are supposed to fill the emotional voids in our lives.

The sudden rash of television programmes like *Big Brother*, with all the attendant tabloid publicity, was greeted by some commentators as a sign of a new downward spiral in the celebrity culture. In the short term, the trend did stimulate a crop of mediocrities into seeking their hour upon the shabby stage. Yet 'Reality TV' looks more like a welcome admission that the celebrity game is almost up. Try as they might, the tabloids and the execrable celebrity magazines can find nothing of any interest to say about the contestants. The attempt to make such people into 'celebrities' has only succeeded in making the notion of celebrity infinitely tedious, because it is too obvious that they are just shameless versions of ourselves. It is hardly surprising that the most successful effort in this genre, *I'm a Celebrity, Get Me Out of Here!*, represented a reversal of the trend because the contestants were already familiar faces to most of the audience. Whatever the source of their fame, most of them had interesting personalities. And unlike the contestants in *Big Brother*, whose lust for

---

[13] Stephen Fry reminds us that the first Director-General of the BBC would not even tolerate the word 'famous'. Lord Reith said that 'If a man is really famous, the word is redundant. If he is not, it is a lie' (Stephen Fry, *Paperweight*, Mandarin edition 1993, 337).

prime-time exposure made them like moths drawn to the light of a blow-torch, those who took part in *I'm a Celebrity* really were under no illusions about the business.[14]

The media's attempt to hollow out the nature of celebrity is part of a more general effort to undermine the concept of loyalty. The self-defeating effects of this trend can be seen in the collapse of a key part of the popular music industry. The turnover of prominent performers has probably always been bewildering to people of a certain age. Now, with the advent of hollow television programmes like *Popstars*, even teenagers must find it hard to keep up. At one time, they were the captive customers of the record labels, who could be confident of a healthy sale for every new release by an established favourite. Nowadays the phrase 'singles market' refers to people in search of a new partner rather than youngsters who spend all week waiting for *Top of the Pops*. Sales have slumped so badly that a record today can reach number one without exceeding a weekly sale of 50,000. In 1979 this would not have secured a place in the top ten.

The media might not mind too much about this particular development; it is, after all, dominated by thirty-somethings who can fill their columns with prattle about the decline of pop from its golden days. But they are not immune from the effects of the decline in loyalty. Like other market actors, the tabloids try to prise away their rivals' customers. Their prime target is the floating reader — a hollow person who has been liberated from 'brand loyalty' and will scan the shelves in search of the most lurid headline or unpleasant photograph. The obvious problem is that these gains are likely to prove temporary. An earth-shattering story about the royal breakfast-ware can net a few hundred thousand extra readers — a worthwhile short-term gain, one might think. But it has to be followed up with a scoop of equal magnitude; otherwise the hollow reader will go back to shopping around for sensation, or even stop visiting the news-agent. If the paper does manage to retain the interest of disloyal

[14] It also should be noted that although *I'm a Celebrity!* tended to be lumped together with Reality shows, there was no pretence that the format was remotely 'realistic'; and no chance that inverted snobs could hail it as an interesting social experiment.

customers, it is likely to be at the cost of irritating those who cling to the idea that a particular publication is 'theirs'. If we were correct in arguing that British prurience is part-time — that the majority actually prefers an occasional break from scaremongering and dirt-dishing — then over time a tabloid will lose at least as many readers as it woos through these tactics. It will be trapped in a vicious circle, struggling to appease a shrinking and increasingly volatile market.[15]

After all, newspapers are not like the commodities which are advertised in their pages. Manufacturers of toothpaste have to face the possibility of a rival promising lower prices, a nicer flavour, or even brighter teeth. But these are not the only hazards for a newspaper editor in a world without loyalty. The packaging, the price and the gimmicky gifts are the easy part. They feel compelled to reinvent their toothpaste every day. Everything depends upon them getting the contents of each issue right — though even they must be dimly aware that this means getting it all drastically wrong. Material gain is the only conceivable compensation for an existence like this — which shows that in one respect, at least, the moral message of the tabloids really does reflect the consistent thinking of those who purvey it.

The career of Piers Morgan, editor of the *Daily Mirror* until May 2004, indicates that reform might be on its way. Unfortunately, it also shows why a radical change is so urgently needed. At the time of his downfall, after publishing faked photographs of alleged British atrocities in Iraq, he was so widely disliked that the other tabloids were deflected momentarily from their persecution of Maxine Carr. But his gross misjudgement should not disguise a more positive contribution. Under his stewardship, the *Mirror* looked as if it was trying to break the dreary tabloid consensus, in which editors competed to drive down standards of public debate. It hardly deserved to be ranked alongside

[15] In April 2004, the *News of the World* tried to use its intrusion into the private life of England's football captain as evidence that it was a paper that could be trusted. The argument seemed to be that one can only trust a newspaper that gets the facts right when it prints stories which undermine trust. The opinion poll response to the Beckham stories suggests that the public felt otherwise.

Mill's *Westminster Review*, and at times it seemed to oppose New Labour just for the sake of making mischief. But at least it was capable of asking awkward questions of a government with an overpowering parliamentary majority and an obsessive mission to appease the right-wing press. Whatever one thinks of its general coverage on Iraq, it performed the crucial democratic function of ensuring that a significant body of public opinion was represented among the tabloids; and it stuck to its line through that brief period when it seemed that the invasion might prosper in accordance with Washington's half-baked plan.

Morgan even made a television series on celebrity which was presented as something of a *mea culpa*, closing with the promise of a change of policy at the *Mirror*. True, this creditable resolution had a limited effect on the content of his newspaper, and Morgan himself never shirked the limelight. But even if one thinks of Morgan as a failed opportunist — *Mirror* sales continued to decline while he was editor — there is something of value in his legacy. At least someone with keen native intelligence and wide experience of the media thought that it would serve his interests to challenge the prevailing tabloid trends.

Ironically, Morgan left the *Mirror* a few days after the newspaper lost a celebrity court-case, against the 'supermodel' Naomi Campbell. By a majority of three to two, the judicial committee of the House of Lords upheld Campbell's complaint that the *Mirror* had infringed her privacy by publishing details of her treatment for drug addiction, even though she had been happy to let the press into her life when it suited her. The decision provoked furious criticism in the press, which felt that the judges had established a privacy law by the back door. In the *Times*, Lord Rees-Mogg savaged both the decision and the way in which it was made. Parliament could have passed a privacy law if it had chosen to do so. Instead, three judges had changed Britain's constitution, and endangered free speech which is 'the foundation of democracy'.[16]

---

[16]   *Times*, 10 May 2004.

Given the cowardice of our elected politicians, a back-door privacy law was the only one we were ever likely to get. But Rees-Mogg was wrong to claim that the Law Lords have revised the constitution without authorisation. They were acting in obedience to the will of parliament. In their ruling they were guided by its decision to pass the 1998 Human Rights Act, which incorporated the European Convention on Human Rights into British law.

The convention protects both privacy (Article 8) and the right to free speech (Article 10). In a fleshed-out society there would be no conflict between these admirable principles, because (for example) the private problems of a supermodel would be a matter of utter indifference for anyone but her close friends and employers.[17] But to us the clash seems obvious, because the press always uses high-flown slogans about 'freedom' to justify its houndings and harassments. And it is safe to predict that in future rulings, the right to individual privacy will prevail more often than not, when set against the right of vast media organisations to make money out of misery.[18] If press behaviour in general had been just a little more responsible, it could expect some public sympathy when it fought legal battles with the likes of Naomi Campbell. Thanks to its own actions, it has transformed the Human Rights Act from an ingenuous wish-list into a potential avenging angel of liberalism.

Taken together, these developments reveal a British media which is in danger of destroying itself — or of acting in a manner which will bring on the destruction of its present practices by means of outside agencies. We have already alluded to the strangely symbiotic relationship between politics and the media in Britain, and we can expect that if hollowed-out liberalism is

---

[17] At the risk of sounding utopian, it might be reasonable to expect that in such a society there would be no 'supermodels' whose privacy could be invaded.

[18] The next important judgement, on the case of Lord Coe, went the other way. The judges in that particular case seemed to think that his adulterous affair was a matter of public interest. Perhaps they have been mixing with the wrong people; or maybe they had an unhealthy obsession with Olympic athletes. Whatever the cause of that idiotic ruling, few judges will care to run the risk of repeating it.

having an impact in one sphere it is likely to be affecting the other. In the next chapter we will look at British politics more closely, to see if the contradictions in the prevailing ideology can help our understanding of recent developments at Westminster and beyond.

Chapter 3

Politics

'OK, wise guy: what do we do now?' Tony Blair to Neil Kinnock, 1 May 1997.[1]

The current state of British politics should require no comment beyond a bare statement of the fact that young people with an interest in current affairs find the media a far more attractive career option. In fact, nowadays the necessary skills are inter-changeable. If they are very lucky, some photogenic politicians might even earn a 'shot at the top' — the chance to host a prime-time television chat show. At the same time, after a life of influencing government decisions without having to take them or stand for election, some media figures condescend to enter the House of Lords (only the masochistic or obscure court humilia-tion by submitting themselves to the voters). And the best part of the deal is that if they keep up their connections with the press they can get paid for contributing their own opinions (which usually means blaming others for their own handiwork). Thus the fangs of the snake have been working away at the political world both from inside and out. In its complete triumph the media can afford to be magnanimous. It has even allowed David Mellor to take a seat in the Last Chance Saloon.

But tempting though it is, this chapter should not turn into a second bout of media-bashing. When we allocate the blame for contemporary troubles, no-one can seriously suggest that politi-cians are as culpable as the tabloids. In retrospect, it is also diffi-cult to see how politicians could have avoided some contamin-

---

[1] Quoted in Andrew Rawnsley, *Servants of the People: The inside story of New Labour*, Penguin edition, 2001, 17.

ation from the hollow, one-dimensional medium of television. Yet they have contrived to make the worst of every difficult situation. For example, they refused permission for the televising of parliamentary proceedings until the place had already fallen into disrepute. The perceptive viewer can now see that the Prime Minister only bothers to attend the Commons for his hollow half-hour of questions. Most important policy decisions are announced in TV studios. Probably the next step will be to turn the Cabinet proceedings into a Big Brother-type reality show. For some members, that would provide a welcome incentive to attend an increasingly-pointless body.

Politicians have added to the bitterness of defeat by denying that it has happened, and by failing to comprehend the nature of the real enemy. Thanks partly to their efforts, the democratic process in Britain has become a mixture of capitulation and confusion, providing the liberal snake with an effective camouflage. We still allow the cliché 'At least Britain is a democracy' to silence every argument, overlooking the fact that it begs all the questions at a time when more than a third of registered voters refuse to participate in the choice of their governors. Such is the persuasive power of liberal slogans even after the essence of liberalism has fled.

One can disagree about the date of the surrender to the snake. Some will trace the decline of parliamentary prestige through the milestones in foreign policy which mark Britain's changing global status since 1945: the end of Empire, the calamitous Suez adventure (1956), and the subsequent half-hearted decision to 'go into Europe'[2] (parliamentary vote 1971, ratified by referendum in 1975). Undoubtedly these developments are part of the story, and the debasement of British politics is clearly linked to a perceived need to distract voters from adverse geopolitical change. In domestic politics, the process can be identified at least as far back as 1950, when the Conservatives chose the irresponsible slogan 'Set the People Free' to explode the residue of wartime comradeship and enlist the spirit of conspicuous consumption

---

[2]   Although, largely thanks to the tabloids, most people seem to think that
       this is a dreadful decision which the British have hitherto avoided.

in the fight against the Attlee Government. In the following decade Labour took its revenge with Wilsonian opportunism, capped by the 1969 Representation of the People Act which extended the franchise to 18 year-olds.[3]

1979 is another key year, when Margaret Thatcher stormed into Downing Street, backed by a troupe of cynical advertisers and image-merchants. At least Mrs Thatcher herself was sincere in her beliefs, and so were some of her senior ministers. But the ideas in themselves were hollow, from her one-dimensional understanding of national sovereignty to her assumption that the unhindered operations of the profit motive always produce the best (and even 'fairest') economic outcomes. This empty view of the world proved more attractive to politicians than to the electorate, which was never more than lukewarm about the Thatcher project and twice re-elected an increasingly triumphalist prime minister with diminishing proportions of their votes. If John Smith had survived long enough to form a government, the process might have stalled. But at the general election three years after his death voters were confronted with two potential parties of government offering almost identical programmes, inspired by the presumed preferences of acquisitive, 'utility-maximising' individuals. Since then the survival of different party labels has seemed increasingly spurious, explicable only by reference to atavistic tribal loyalties. Of the three main groupings, only the Liberal Democrats approximate even remotely to 'fleshed-out' liberalism. But the suspicion that things might change if the party came close to winning anything of significance will have struck any witness to the behaviour of its activists during closely-fought by-elections.

Whatever the reasons and the cast of culprits, it is possible to read the political history of post-war Britain as a transition from fleshed-out to hollowed-out liberalism. In itself, this process has had the lamentable effect of depriving voters of a meaningful choice of government. But that is not the end of the bad news.

---

[3] Despite the fact that an all-party group had recommended 20 as a compromise.

The hollow creed which now dominates the British political scene is not really a philosophy of government at all.

We argued earlier that Isaiah Berlin's distinction between 'negative' and 'positive' liberty is seriously misleading if we want to understand the work of the greatest liberal writers. Their primary concern was with the development of the individual, not with the extent of state intervention. Yet in the contemporary context there is a connection between Berlin's categories and our own concepts of 'fleshed-out' and 'hollowed-out' liberalism. Fleshed-out liberals tend to follow John Maynard Keynes (1883–1946) and William Beveridge (1879–1963), in thinking that the state can play a constructive role in reducing the element of economic insecurity in the lives of British citizens. On Berlin's criteria, this makes them believers in 'positive' liberty and thus potential enemies of freedom.

Although this debate goes to the heart of liberal disagreements about the nature of rationality and individual fulfilment, it is essential to note that there is no *necessary* connection between 'fleshed-out' liberalism and 'positive' liberty. Keynes and Beveridge believed that economic insecurity was a handicap to individual development, and thought that it could be reduced by state action in a way that would increase the sum total of individual liberty. They were responding to the violent fluctuations of the inter-war economy, which made it impossible for liberals to argue that there was any connection between a sense of security and individual merit. In other words, they were practically-minded men who wanted to preserve a liberal society, and thought that only an interventionist state could do this in the circumstances of their time. If the inter-war world had been different, suggesting that unregulated capitalism really was the best means to ensure individual fulfilment for the overwhelming majority of citizens, their policy proposals would have been quite different.

The fleshed-out followers of Beveridge and Keynes still believe in the principle of an interventionist state, for reasons that will be discussed in the final section. But if they were consistent, they would welcome any sign that the scope of state activity could be 'rolled back' without reintroducing unacceptable levels of insecurity.[4] They would rejoice, for example, if citizens recognised David Selbourne's 'Principle of Duty' to the extent that the voluntary sector could develop the capacity to take on some of the functions currently dominated by the state. By contrast, although they might differ in the degree of their hostility, hollowed-out liberals can only be antagonistic towards the modern state. They hate it when it stops them speeding in their beloved motor-cars, or imposes taxation to help the environment. They resent the benefits it gives to other people, and part of them even feels uneasy when they suck in benefits for themselves, in the form of free schooling or health care. They want it to go away and leave them to do what comes naturally, within the limits imposed by an ample contingent of police and prison officers. They will only recognise the voluntary principle when those guardians of the consumerist order prove inadequate. During his celebrated spell as Home Secretary (1993–7), Michael Howard cited 130,000 Neighbourhood Watch schemes and 20,000 special constables as 'the clearest demonstration that community spirit in Britain is alive and well and full of potential'.[5] This is like saying that an increase in army recruitment can be taken as a symptom of international tranquillity.

The British still like to see themselves as volunteers in constructive causes rather than gung-ho vigilantes; and by the same token they do not take state-hating to US levels. But in order to retain a generally positive view of the state as a useful instrument of the civic order they have to ignore the contrary message purveyed by large sections of the media, and by too many of their politicians. Take, for example, the organisation which is still known as the 'Conservative Party'. Conservative politicians

---

[4] By the same token, they were aghast after Mrs Thatcher's Bruges speech in which she boasted about having rolled back the frontiers of the British state. She had done no such thing. The policy framework designed by Beveridge and Keynes provided some security for the people who lost their jobs during the two Thatcherite recessions; and although her governments privatised much of the state sector, it took interference to unprecedented lengths in other respects, notably the bullying of local government and the procedures of the teaching profession (see Simon Jenkins, *Accountable to None: The Tory nationalization of Britain*, Hamish Hamilton, 1995).

[5] *Times*, 16 August 1994.

still bang on about Edmund Burke and occasionally decorate their speeches with a selective quotation. But if they actually read his *Reflections* they would be amazed to find him arguing that 'the state ought not to be considered as nothing better than a partnership agreement in a trade of pepper and coffee, callico or tobacco, or some other such low concern'[6].

Now, Burke was incapable of ordering his breakfast without committing some rhetorical excess. So we need not follow him either in denigrating those who deal in coffee and calico, or in regarding the state as the instrument of some divine purpose. But we should give careful consideration to his notion that market transactions and the activities of the state belong in different categories. To do otherwise calls into question the legitimacy of the state and its agents, when (for example) they claim the right to regulate the market, let alone to wage war abroad or even to defend citizens against threats to domestic security.

Members of the contemporary Conservative Party do not confuse the activities of the state with market transactions. In their view that would be too high a compliment to the state. In other words, they are precisely the kind of people that Burke was trying to warn about. A sly dig at the state is compulsory for any speaker at a party conference who wants a standing ovation. A Conservative who wants to establish a reputation as a 'thinker' need only proclaim that the over-mighty state should be rolled back, reined in, or removed from the backs of the people. In a peculiar personal statement of principle published as a full-page article in the *Times*, Michael Howard recently proclaimed his belief 'That the people should be big. That the state should be small'.[7] Even the Europhobes who speak loudest of 'sovereignty' attack the functions of the British state under the indiscriminate umbrella of 'bureaucracy'. In practice, of course, the Conservatives suffered from a rage for regulation while they were in office. But they found a way of doing this at arms-length, through semi-autonomous agencies which were more than semi-stuffed with their own friends from the business world.

[6]   Edmund Burke, *Reflections on the Revolution in France*, Penguin edition, 1969, 194.

[7]   *Times*, 2 January 2004.

Surely things are different in the Labour Party, addicted as it supposedly is to the policies of 'tax and spend' (whatever that means)? True, Gordon Brown apparently retains some faith in the constructive role of the state. But even he rarely preaches what he practices. To judge from his rhetoric, we owe his attack on child poverty to 'Labour', or 'prudence', rather than the state. He is, after all, a fervent admirer of (most) things American, and has an inexplicable attachment to the Private Finance Initiative (PFI). While Brown damns the state by his silence, Tony Blair is an open and noisy critic. For him the state is the final refuge of the 'forces of conservatism' (by which, of course, he means the opponents of change, rather than the official Opposition). His determination to talk about a 'Third Way' rather than identifying himself with social democracy is largely due to his fear of being labelled a 'statist' by his fair-weather friends in the tabloid press. Recently even the Liberal Democrats have joined in the game, taking up the Thatcherite dream of abolishing the Department of Trade and Industry. Positive feelings towards the state have become the political equivalent of paedophilia.

Academics have noticed the recent trend towards 'hollowing out' the institutions of the British state, through membership of the European Union, devolution and the growth of the quango-cracy. But this process is merely a symptom of a more insidious development. The general acceptance by British politicians of the moronic mantra 'private good, public bad' means that even where the state is still active it is under an implied threat from its elected masters. At present, the parties have agreed to except the NHS (and 'bog-standard' schools) from the suspended sentence. But senior politicians only sound remotely sincere when they are questioning the performance of any state agency. Trying to laugh off the fiasco of the Millennium Dome, Tony Blair said that it was ridiculous to expect a better outcome when the state tries to run a tourist attraction. In fact, not even a combination of Henry Ford and Billy Butlin could have made a success of the Dome, which was an idiotic idea dreamed up by Michael Heseltine, then endorsed by Blair in an early exhibition of execrable judgement. But Blair's throw-away line revealed more than his capacity for guilt-displacement. If the state should keep its hands off one (admittedly expensive) tourist venue, it has no right to meddle with an organisation as vast and as serious as the NHS.

Even after Brown's recent spending splurges, the public sector accounts for less than 42 per cent of Britain's GDP, compared to an EU average which is more than 5 per cent higher. But the sums involved are still enormous. Where does all the money go? The present government, like the last one, is keen to talk about 'waste' in the context of welfare-malingerers and unnecessary pen-pushers. They are more reticent on the subject of the privatisation-peddlers in the City of London — who receive a fat commission every time a national asset is sold off cheaply to a favoured bidder — or the computer firms who are paid in full even when their products fail to function, and the defence-industry drones who provide 'hi-tech' equipment which is more lethal to the user than the enemy. For obvious reasons, the media is happy to help the government hush up these scandals. In the same spirit Thatcher's privatisation programme was hailed as a triumph for popular capitalism, rather than a wholesale give-away of undervalued assets which would end up benefiting multi-national corporations rather than the beguiled average punter.

Amid all the current talk of directing government funds towards 'front-line services', these unpleasant auxiliaries in the private sector will continue to dip into taxpayers pockets. Thanks to the PFI, 'entrepreneurial' private companies will still be receiving risk-free subventions when New Labour itself is as outdated as Keir Hardie's cap. None of this would have happened if the government had recognised the necessity to define a new role for the state after its landslide victory in 1997. Its failure to do so implies that although the electorate has been post-Thatcherite since the mid-1980s at the latest, our governors are still encumbered with a mindset which equates 'waste' with 'undeserved benefits for the poor', while regarding generous subsidies for the private sector as a justified use for the public purse.

If Burke was even half right, politicians who still extract more than forty per cent of a nation's wealth in taxation should be desperate to avoid making their profession seem like a 'low con-

cern'. Yet this is the inevitable effect of their scoffing pronounce-
ments on the competence of the state. Why, then, do they do it?
The phenomenon arises from a mixture of primitive instinct,
acquired habit and short-sighted calculation. The first prompts
them to lash out at those who are least able to retaliate — the typical response of people suffering from fragile self-esteem. The
second is a continuation of the Thatcherite tendency to pick a
quarrel with someone when everything else seems to be failing.
The third tells them that this particular quarrel will endear them
to the electorate, and to their sponsors in the business community. It will help them achieve the real purpose of political life,
which is to keep winning elections until the time comes to retire
to some opulent boardroom.

We saw in the previous section that the press has undermined
itself, by focusing its appeal on footloose consumers who shop
around for satisfaction. In the quest for a larger market share,
newspapers have pandered to this audience with features which
repel their more reliable readers. British politicians are now
exhibiting the same fatal tendency. Attacking the state in order
to improve one's chances of running it is obviously self-
defeating; it is like chopping off one's legs in order to fashion a
nice new pair of stilts. But politicians will grasp at any expedient
which promises to improve their stature. The more they plum-
met in public esteem, the more that they long to be loved. It is
hardly surprising that they rivet their full attention on the one
popularity poll which, to date, has always been won by a group
of politicians.

There has never been a golden age of elections — either before
or after universal adult suffrage. But there certainly was a time,
not so long ago, when candidates could slip the occasional hollow promise or meaningless slogan into their campaign pitches
without losing all respect for themselves and others. At that time
elections were a means to a constructive end. Some might have
regarded them as a regrettable necessity, others as a chance to
campaign on behalf of sincerely held beliefs. But once the polls
had closed, there was a settled understanding that elected politicians of all parties would deliberate on issues of national importance without playing to the gallery. They might have to seek the

support of some hollowed-out voters in order to win a place in parliament; but once they were there they behaved as if they were legislating for a fleshed-out public.

This benign approach to politics breaks down when the main focus shifts from the end to the means: when people begin to regard the conduct of government as nothing more than a way to win the next election. Perpetual campaigning is damaging enough in itself. It makes political life a struggle which ceases only in retirement or in premature, stress-induced death — a prospectus which can only appeal to hollowed-out Hobbesians. But politicians have made matters even worse, by allowing social scientists, spin-doctors and advertising gurus to dictate their tactical thinking, at and between elections. In order to win and retain power they are told that they must target 'floating voters', who are presumed to act in accordance with 'rational choice', which consists of our hollow friends: acquisitive individualism and short-term self-interest. The beauty of this model is that it claims to fit everyone — the faithful and the fickle alike — because it reduces all motivation to the same standard. The snag is that it represents, at best, a hollow mutation from the old liberal theory of human nature. Yet, as we saw above, that liberal tradition is still providing the high-sounding slogans which we hear when politicians want to defend contemporary democratic practices.

The New Labour project can be summarised as an attempt to track down the hollow voter and give him what he wants. Some government supporters complain that there is inadequate coverage of its concrete achievements in domestic affairs.[8] Yet this is no accident. It is characteristic of the liberal snake in political action. Although economic inequality has widened to the satisfaction of anyone who wants to 'Bring Home the Revolution', the poor have certainly benefited from measures like the minimum wage and the Working Families' Tax Credit. But all this has to be done by stealth, in case it offends Mandevillian Man. The government's presentational energies are focused on areas where it might be vulnerable to criticism from the 'rational'

---

[8]   The *Guardian* columnist Polly Toynbee is (in all respects) the best example.

voter. Such a person, it is assumed, will not be impressed by honest admissions of failure; he will have no time for losers, and barely understands the concepts of honesty or loyalty. The state, he has been told, is just a drain on his pay- packet. Creative misuse of statistics is the only way to keep him quiet, until the next election is over and the endless campaign enters a new phase.

So when ministers are presented with policy alternatives, the lust for instant results drives out any consideration of long-term interest. The public is deluged with pledge-cards, initiatives, tsars, targets, task-forces and league tables, whether they want them or not. Promises are 'delivered' when complex problems can be stuffed into convincing statistical packages and sold with a sound-bite. Some departments continue to strive for concrete results, while others are content to hand over all responsibility to the spin-doctors. As a result, the process of government becomes more incoherent than ever before. A process which began as an attempt to appease the bureaucrat-baiting individual ends up with more unproductive people on the payroll than ever before, in the scramble to provide positive presentation. Nowadays, in the age of tabloid politics, this is called 'joined-up government'.

New Labour might think it can keep winning elections with its coalition of the benighted and the partially-satisfied. On a narrow perspective it could be right. But it has already suffered the heaviest political defeat in British history. If the genuine enthusiasm which greeted its landslide win in 1997 was eloquent testimony to pent-up public demand for a return to fleshed-out politics, the twelve per cent fall in turnout four years later marked the extent to which expectations had been disappointed. New Labour had a vested interest in disbelieving any evidence of euphoria in the aftermath of its first victory. If there had been some substance behind it, the party's strategists would have had to admit that they had spent the previous three years posing the wrong questions to their hollow focus groups. Those bodies were set up to validate New Labour's assumption that the election would be decided by people who could only experience strong emotions when they bought a new car or opened a copy of *Loaded* magazine. Tony Blair's response was to promise that having campaigned as New Labour, he would govern as New

Labour. If any lucid meaning can be attached to these words, it translates as, 'I have sought the votes of hollow people, and I will govern for hollow people'. It was a promise to govern for people much like himself; and, to give him credit, Blair has not let himself down.

The mass abstentions of 2001 were a predictable response to this depressing denouement to the Thatcher years. They might be only the beginning. Turnout is at its highest among older voters, who have been unable to shake off partisan loyalties forged in the days of fleshed-out politics. As these generations troop off to the polling booth in the sky, they leave behind an increasing proportion of floating voters. Even on the optimistic assumption that fleshed-out individuals will remain a numerical majority of the electorate, the outlook is grim. These people will be least likely to vote unless they are given reasons to respect or trust the leading contestants; and the main parties are determined to act as if these emotions are illusory. Thus the argument that the 'ration- al' hollowed-out voter wields a decisive electoral influence becomes a self-fulfilling prophecy; and the quality of debate, decisions and the characters of the politicians themselves can only head in one direction.

Given the weight of evidence, our politicians have been forced to acknowledge that they are somewhat unpopular. But, as in the case of the media, their proposed remedies can only make matters worse. Voting is to be made easier — an initiative which will drag in a few more frivolous punters, while leaving untouched the growing proportion who have started to abstain out of principle.

It is also suggested that the franchise should be extended to sixteen year-olds. The only conceivable justification for such a move is that it will educate a new electoral cohort, nurturing the voting habit. But British democracy today is like a school in which the teachers queue up to congratulate the pupils on their precocious erudition, and assure them that they have nothing more to learn.[9] In important areas of life, where most people

[9] The analogy with schools is also pertinent because New Labour was hoping to lower the voting age while trying to encourage sixteen year-olds

could do with some guidance, British politicians of every party compete to flatter a 'mature' electorate which is eager to exercise 'choice'.[10] Immune to evidence or rudimentary logic, opposition leaders have become more gushing than ever in praising the sagacity of the British public, while their chances really depend on a mass realisation that voters have allowed themselves to be duped by the Blairites. It might be true, as Kate Figgis has argued, that teenagers today are more sensitive and wily than their elders.[11] If so, it would be wise to protect them from the electoral process for as long as possible. But a poll of 5,000 teenagers published in March 2004 suggested that 'they are tough on crime and bogus asylum seekers, oppose abortion and the legalisation of soft drugs, support the pound, ID cards, marriage and the monarchy and mistrust the European Union'.[12] This sounds like a tabloid generation, whose thinking is unlikely to change when they are old enough to vote. We ought to give serious consideration to means of staving off the evil hour for as long as possible, and raise the voting age to twenty-one.

The main casualty of the imbecilic electoral auction is the standing of the British state. Yet politicians still suffer from an interventionist itch. They can try to enforce 'choice' by meddling with the public services; elsewhere they can prevent it, by cracking down on hunters, smokers and smackers. Having relinquished control of the economy to the spiritual prostitutes of the money-markets, they fight in the last ditch against the free movement of people. Torn between the desire to act the bully and the compulsion to flatter, the parties have become obsessed with the idea that the electorate regards them as 'out of touch with real people'. Common sense suggests that this recurrent

---

to prolong their education — presumably on the assumption that a couple more years gaining knowledge would equip them for adult life. The maximum incentive offered by the Department of Education and Skills was a payment of £30 per week, while the guaranteed minimum wage for those who decided to leave school at sixteen was £112. Joined-up government gets no better than this.

[10] As John Gray has written, success in our political culture apparently 'depends on flattering the electorate while mobilising its baser instincts': *New Statesman*, 10 November 2003.

[11] *The Terrible Teens: What every parent needs to know*, Penguin, 2004.

[12] Survey for *Bliss* magazine, reported in *Times*, 11 March 2004.

opinion-poll finding is simply a short-hand way of expressing disagreement with a range of policy decisions, or disgust with politicians who take turns in belittling their own profession. But in the bizarre world of the British political party it has been interpreted as a reason for developing an even better understanding of the hollowed-out 'rational actor' — a pseudo-academic construct, whose unwelcome intrusion caused most of the trouble in the first place.

In a healthy democratic state — one, for example, which really could boast of its own virtues while displacing foreign regimes that operate by different standards — a turnout of less than sixty per cent in a general election would be regarded as a national catastrophe. It should have been no less disturbing in a liberal democracy than the revelation that only a sixth of newspaper purchasers trust what they read. But political parties have been insulated from the shock of the 2001 general election. Our elected representatives may be profligate, but the running costs of the democratic show are relatively trivial. And parties no longer need contributions from a mass membership when a few wealthy individuals are happy to meet the shortfall. Public demand is falling, and the products all look the same: but these developments make a political investment more tempting than ever.

One hates to generalise, and there are still some people who love democracy enough to stave off the bankruptcy of parties whose disappearance would be detrimental to the body politic. Yet others clearly regard a donation as a debt which must be settled after the election, and are ready to take their custom elsewhere in case of default. At the very least, these patrons are paying for guaranteed private access to their hired helpers. This is behaviour that the politicians can recognise, after all those years of searching for 'Mondeo Man', 'Worcester Women', and all those ghoulish products of the alliterative imagination. The proceeds give them a chance to surround themselves with kindred souls — those misfits who would like to be Machiavellian but are nothing more than Mandelsonian, spinning and fixing their way to safe seats, a place in the new-look 'House of Lords' or an occasional guest appearance on a commercial radio phone-in during the graveyard slot.

Readers of Plato cannot have missed a resemblance between our own circumstances and the worst excesses of Athenian democracy. Plato was not particularly troubled by 'ordinary' people who based their everyday decisions on opinion rather than knowledge. They would be quite harmless were it not for their flatterers, who convinced them that their half-baked ideas should be decisive in public affairs. We hold no brief for the Conservative Party, which has been the post-war trend-setter in this respect and has learned no lessons through its years out of office. But New Labour's leaders and functionaries bear an unsettling resemblance to the sophists of Socratic nightmare. For them there is no pausing place between lofty ideals and the lowest common denominator. They have parallels in modern European history as well as ancient Greece. With no home and no history, the Blairites have tried to purge our memories of everything that happened before 1997 in a genuflection towards the most tawdry of the French Revolutionaries. Robespierre and Danton would have been impressed by Blair's treatment of the House of Lords, which he ripped apart before he had thought how to design a new institution to serve his interests.

Plato and other classical writers who warned about the dangers of democracy deserve to be treated seriously today. Like the arguments of Burke, their objections apply with additional force in the contemporary setting, since our societies are much more difficult to manage than the small-scale city states where the democratic system was first tried with such mixed results. Yet the present argument is not so defeatist. There is no reason to suppose that human nature is too flawed to allow democracy to work at any time. There is, though, plenty of evidence to suggest that universal suffrage can be implemented prematurely, in an inappropriate context, for reasons which have more to do with political opportunism than an attention to real developments in a fast-changing society. And once full democracy has been implemented at the wrong time, there can be no going back.

This is one respect in which the idea of 'Bringing Home the Revolution' might make some sense. Back in the eighteenth cen-

tury the Americans were wise enough to institute a written constitution, with clear divisions between the three branches of
government. They had the advantage on us, because their
'Founding Fathers' like Alexander Hamilton knew all about the
dangers of hollowed-out liberalism from the outset: it is, after
all, the American ethos. As we know, the separation of powers in
the US has failed to withstand the weight of perceived public
opinion. But a similar system might work in Britain, if it could be
introduced at the right time. The problem is that after years of
well-meaning proposals from fleshed-out liberals — and even
from one of Thatcher's Cabinet ministers, Lord Hailsham, while
his party was out of power in the 1970s — constitutional reform
is being given a bad name by Tony Blair's attempt to ensure the
permanent dictatorship of Mondeo Man.

Anyone who senses a touch of exaggeration in the foregoing
account would do well to consider Blair's refusal to apply one
simple institutional remedy that might arrest the downward
spiral. He almost committed his party to proportional representation before the 1997 general election. But his enthusiasm
declined after a measly forty-three per cent of those who voted
left him with the largest parliamentary majority since the
National Government of 1931. A proportional result in 1997
would actually have strengthened the hand of a far-sighted
Prime Minister; with a smaller majority in the Commons it
would have been easier to deal with potential dissidents, and
less tempting to embark on irrational adventures.

Before 1997 Blair had taken on powerful vested interests
within the Labour Party, in his campaign to trade the totemic
Clause IV for a piece of pretentious verbiage. But he baulked at
the prospect of a second contest, which would have secured a
tangible prize. His refusal to act on the findings of his own
Jenkins Commission stands as a poetic contrast to his eager
acceptance of House of Lords reform. In the one case there was a
pressing need for change, and a considered plan of action; in the
other, the institution had been performing its allotted role with
amazing competence, and all the favoured options were half-
baked. Blair's decision to smash the Lords and shelve Jenkins
does not rule out the possibility that at some point in the

medium term PR could be introduced as a matter of principle for general elections. All the best arguments against it apply with equal force to the present political environment, which already discriminates heavily against elected representatives who prefer the dictates of their own consciences to the demands of central party discipline. It offers at least a theoretical chance of improvement, which is more than one can say for first-past-the-post. The right system would encourage well-informed and principled voters back into a process which currently leaves them no meaningful choice, unless they live in a constituency where tactical voting could make a constructive difference, or they wish to make an expression of loyalty towards an individual candidate who has managed to retain some 'fleshed-out' features.

PR continues to hover at the edges of the politically possible because it attacks hollowed-out liberals at their most vulnerable point. They can scarcely argue against a system which brings the outcome of elections closer to the real preferences of the people. A reformed voting system would be the perfect solution to the mess over the House of Lords, but this cannot be contemplated because it would give the second Chamber the moral authority which the Commons has lost. So they simply vote it down and hope (in true tabloid style) that the public will forget about it. More radical changes are excluded from debate, because they offend against our cherished pre-suppositions; they seem to be retrograde steps, as if it were still remotely possible to regard history as some kind of linear progression. One man who did believe in progress, John Stuart Mill, argued for the retention of public voting — the open declaration of preference on the hustings. Contemporary liberals refer to Mill's position with regret, as evidence that even the greatest of minds can malfunction. Yet the main argument in favour of the secret ballot — the possibility of intimidation by vested interests — has much less force today, when political preferences must be a long way down the list of potential reasons for workplace insecurity.[13] Fear of intimida-

---

[13] Mill, indeed, thought that they were a minimal concern even before open voting was abolished in 1872.

tion has not stopped Labour from holding all-postal ballots in local government and European elections, although under this procedure there is more chance that the intimidation will remain undetected (not to mention the chance it gives for other kinds of fraud). A return to public voting would at least force the hypocritical anti-heroes of 'the spiral of silence' (if they really exist) out into the open; and it has more chance of reinvigorating the stale ceremonies of election day than the various types of 'distance' voting via internet or the Royal Mail.

But while public voting might make life more uncomfortable for the hollowed-out elector, there is another measure which, if practicable, could banish him entirely. In recent contributions to the debate Gordon Graham and Keith Sutherland have argued that 'competence testing' should apply to political participation as it does in other fields like the law and medicine.[14] It is a sign of how badly our democracy has gone astray that this idea would be regarded as wildly implausible by most politicians. The same people would be incensed by a proposal to abolish the driving test. In fact, that process has recently been amended to make it more difficult to pass. The presumption here is that it is dangerous to allow unqualified persons to sit unsupervised at the wheel of a motor vehicle; but it is perfectly acceptable to entice individuals into the democratic process, even if they are utterly ignorant of or indifferent to the issues at stake. Few politicians have responded to the problems on British roads by arguing that the age at which one can legally drive should be lowered, without any proof of competence; yet this is their new answer to widespread political apathy.

If there were any reliable method of measuring IQ, that could be introduced as a satisfactory indicator of competence. For more sceptical souls, a series of questions about the policies of the main parties would suffice, together with a comprehension exercise based on the proceedings of a recent standing committee. The questions ought to be difficult, and would have to be phrased in a manner which excluded the possibility of lucky

[14]   Gordon Graham, *The Case Against the Democratic State*, Imprint Academic, 2002; Keith Sutherland, *The Party's Over: Blueprint for a very English revolution*, Imprint Academic, 2004.

guesses. But the qualifying rate must not be too demanding. The rationale behind such a test would be to deter those who have no more than a casual interest in politics even from applying for a vote. Some unpleasant fanatics would slip through, of course; but if we believe that knowledgeable British moderates are out-numbered by well-informed extremists, we really have given up on our country.[15]

Unfortunately, even if this idea were to win a serious hearing there would be a serious practical difficulty. In a society which rewards perceived outcomes rather than real achievement, widespread cheating could undermine the whole process. At present our elections depend on the honesty of volunteers who oversee the casting of votes and the subsequent counting, so it would hardly demand a giant leap of faith to trust those who adjudicate on political competence. But there would be a danger of the tests being leaked in advance. At a time when so many people treat the right to vote so lightly, it might seem ludicrous to expect that anyone would take the trouble of paying for the chance of a sneaky glimpse. But recent scandals involving exam-ination papers show that it can and will be done if people have a sufficient motive; and if the right to vote becomes more exclu-sive, that incentive will increase for private individuals — not to mention unscrupulous politicians who cannot hope to win much support through fair play.

These doubts reflect a general problem with institutional or procedural remedies of a truly radical nature. They tend to put the cart before the horse, and would only be workable if the problem to be tackled was already in abeyance. Reforms which would work admirably in a fleshed-out society are unlikely to help us out of our existing hollow environment; they would only stand a chance of being implemented in the wake of a national conflagration, which we should hope to avoid. This observation

---

[15] Here I should be understood as using the terms 'moderate' and 'extreme' in an absolute rather than a relative sense. Some of the policies passed by successive governments since 1974 have been pretty 'extreme' by any sane standard. Equally, one would anticipate some radical changes in the present policy structure if MPs were elected under the voting system recommended here; but only victims of the snake could think of them as 'extreme'.

applies to Sutherland's most radical suggestion: that the people's representatives should be chosen by lot, like a jury, rather
than by any form of voting. Equally, the Californian practice of
'recalling' representatives would be worth supporting if one
could have confidence that the required proportion of voters
would show responsibility in exercising that power, and would
not merely use it to elect another fading muscle-bound film star.
PR and open voting are suggested here for the more modest purpose of slowing the rot. In the absence of more fundamental
changes of attitude, they are unlikely to stop it. So fixed-term
parliaments, at four-yearly intervals, should be added to the list.
Since 1945, only one general election has been called indisput-
ably for honourable reasons before the five-year term expired.
On that occasion Clement Attlee's Labour Party was defeated, as
was the Conservative Party in February 1974, when Edward
Heath was acting honourably when he called a snap election
(even if some of his advisers were not). The Prime Ministerial
prerogative of demanding an early dissolution of parliament is
indefensible now that elections are called every four years
(unless the government is trying to delay an inevitable defeat, or
has mishandled some bovine disorder). Fixed four-yearly terms
have hardly banished cynical manipulation from US elections.
But in the absence of a clear division of powers in Britain, it cannot be right that the Prime Minister can manipulate the date of
the election when he or she already has so much influence over
the conduct of the campaign itself. There should be a provision
for early elections, but only if it proves impossible to assemble a
majority government from the existing parliament.

The piecemeal reforms suggested here are not intended as a
replacement for a more radical overhaul. Rather, they would be
a necessary prelude to the kind of debate from which an overall
constitutional settlement could arise. Although few of them will
feel able to agree, reforms along these lines would benefit British
politicians. In his *Reflections* Burke warned that 'The degree of
estimation in which any profession is held becomes the standard
of estimation in which the professors hold themselves'. By an
agreeable topical coincidence, Burke was referring to an assem-
bly which had granted too much influence to second-rate law-

yers. But his words apply to most of today's British legislators, whatever their professional backgrounds. He was equally pertinent when he wrote that 'Flattery corrupts both the receiver and the giver'.[16] It is hardly surprising that the compulsory, insincere sycophancy which disfigures British elections has resulted in a level of public contempt which is beginning to seep back into Westminster itself. This can only lend weight to the arguments of right-wing 'libertarians', who despise the state as the last obstacle to a Hobbesian 'war of all against all' (from which they are clearly confident that they will emerge victorious).

The chief tragedy of politics in Britain today is that few politicians really deserve the mockery with which the public greets their endeavours. It is truly remarkable that a group of essentially well-meaning people should have contrived to generate so much public scorn. Most MPs and parliamentary candidates of all parties are fleshed-out liberals, who have been forced to reach an accommodation with an imaginary enemy because their parties are dominated by an obsession with 'floating voters'. Even if they are indeed out of touch with many aspects of the 'real' world, they certainly know all about the strains imposed by an excessive work-load, and the misery that accompanies a thankless life. Tony Blair himself probably would have remained a 'Pretty Straight Guy' if he had only realised in good time that a great Prime Minister needs more than a doe-eyed expression and the gift of the gab.[17]

The decision of MPs to vote themselves a salary increase, and thus a better pension, just before the 1997 election made so many of them redundant, must surely rank highest among their self-defeating gestures. The petty corruption of a few of their number in the 1990s, enveloped in the blanket-term 'sleaze', bears no comparison. But in a response which was typical of the brave new pluralistic Britain, the unelected media forced the appoint-

---

[16] Burke, *Reflections*, 130, 90.
[17] Blair called himself 'a pretty straight sort of guy' to excuse himself from involvement in a party funding scandal shortly after he became a pristine Prime Minister in 1997. See Nick Cohen's *Pretty Straight Guys*, Faber and Faber, 2003, for a devastating critique (which is strangely at odds with the author's support for the war on Iraq).

ment of a committee to monitor the operations of democracy. The result was the establishment of a Committee on Standards in Public Life (1994), which decreed that elected politicians should be more virtuous than most other members of society. In a hollow relic of the old public service ethos, MPs who surrender their integrity to the whips in the hope of party preferment now deliver pompous rebukes to colleagues who have failed to give a full declaration of their outside interests.

British MPs must be almost alone in accepting their bad name before mounting the gallows. It is they, and not the public, who need to be saved from themselves. Their best chance would be to kick against the hollow system of modern party discipline. On this score, recent developments which have been depressing enough in the short term might turn out to be much more positive. The whips office was strained to the limit in John Major's second term, as the government struggled to win key votes on European integration. Labour's bloated parliamentary majority has been obedient enough; the government even won the vote on university tuitions fees, in defiance of its own manifesto promises. Yet the ties have been loosened through a series of unsuccessful rebellions. As always in human affairs, a mixture of motives has been at work in the process. But the overall effect might be a decline of deference in the one area of British life where this might actually bring beneficial results.

Chapter 4

The Public Services

Those who serve in large governmental agencies or departments are, it is thought, an inferior part of the citizenry.... as individuals, they may be diligent, personable and socially useful. Collectively they are stolid, incompetent and, above all, a burden on the society. They are 'bureaucrats' — John Kenneth Galbraith, 1992.[1]

Philip Gould ranks high among the architects of New Labour. One of Michael Oakeshott's more unlikely students at the London School of Economics, he joined the Labour Party at 15 and has played a key role in campaigning since 1985. Drawing inspiration from American techniques, he became an enthusiast for 'Bringing Home the Revolution', organising focus groups and offering confidential tactical advice which sometimes fell into mischievous hands. He is not an infallible judge of public opinion; in 1997 he doubted that Labour would win at all until almost the last minute. According to Tony Blair's biographer, he only changed his mind after consulting 'a group of eight women from Watford'.[2]

After the voters of Watford helped to return a record number of Labour MPs, Gould emerged from his backstairs station and published a book about the transformation of the party. It was seen as an invaluable guide to electoral success, not least by the Conservative Party leader, William Hague who circulated copies among his front-bench team. Gould recounted his feelings of

[1]   *The Culture of Contentment*, Sinclair-Stevenson, 1992, 70.
[2]   John Rentoul, *Tony Blair: Prime Minister*, Little, Brown, 2001, 313.

anguish in the 1980s as 'old' Labour failed the British people. The party 'had offered education, choices and opportunities, but the people had turned on them.' And for good reason:

> Labour had failed to understand that the old working class was becoming a new middle class: aspiring, consuming, choosing what was best for them and their families. They had outgrown crude collectivism and left it behind in the supermarket car-park.[3]

On the same page, Gould begins a brief account of his formative influences. He salutes the memory of his father, 'a fine and talented man who would have made a success of any career he chose.' He was, though, somewhat careless of his appearance; 'not out of laziness or lack of aptitude, but simply because he did not care about the ordinary workings of physical things.' This outlook fitted him perfectly for the career he had chosen, from the limitless range of opportunity for which his talents had equipped him. He was a teacher, with a mission 'to transform the lives of the children in his care'. In other words, Mr Gould senior was a dedicated public servant.[4]

Gould's account of his father is written with genuine feeling. But the reader cannot help noticing an element of unconscious irony. Possibly the elder Gould hoped that his tender charges would end up as selfish materialists, and relished the prospect that one day they would live under a government which understood and encouraged their acquisitive impulses. But one rather doubts it. Gould informs us that his father's politics were 'non-conformist, individualistic, Liberal'. Perhaps the father held beliefs which contradicted his practice, but again there is reason to be sceptical. More likely, he lived at a time when liberal individualism meant something more than naked self-interest. The real contradiction can be found in his son, who has been quite happy to base electoral calculations on assumptions about

---

[3]   Philip Gould, *The Unfinished Revolution: How the modernisers saved the Labour Party*, Little, Brown, 1998, 4.

[4]   *Ibid.*, 4-5.

human beings which would have horrified his father. Yet he continues to see himself as a humble servant in the same cause.[5]

Philip Gould feels that an apology is in order on behalf of his parents because they 'wanted to do what was right, not what was aspirational'.[6] This distinction is a bit of a slip from a New Labour guru, who must surely think that to be 'right' is the same as being 'aspirational'. But unlike his modern counterparts Gould's father could set these rival priorities at their true value. He didn't need to worry that his shoes were 'never quite clean', or that he used a paper-clip to hold his spectacles together.[7] Fashionable accessories were less important to him than respect: respect for himself, and respect received from others in recognition of his work. Since his day, public servants have been deprived of this non-material reward for their efforts. Today's public servants do have aspirations; but instead of hoping for riches, most of them merely want the chance to get on with their jobs, free from unnecessary disturbances. They still feel that they ought to do what is right, but they are running desperately short of reasons.

Nothing typifies the modern, hollowed-out politician better than his attitude towards the public services. In Britain it was strongly positive up to the 1970s. Governments of all parties readily assumed that public servants lived up to their name — that they were strongly motivated to work in the national interest. In Philip Gould's terminology, they were guilty of 'crude collectivism'. The experience of two world wars cemented the reputation of state servants. They were seen as the essential organisers of victory. The only dissenters from this positive picture were Labour's left-wingers, who were convinced that senior civil servants had an agenda which they took no trouble to conceal. They were all part of the 'Establishment', with a vested interest in squashing radical reforms at birth. But these criticisms were confined to the top ranking officials. When even miners in the nationalised coal industry were civil servants of a

---

[5]   Not so humble, now. He was elevated to the peerage while this essay was being revised for publication.
[6]   *Ibid.*, 4.
[7]   *Ibid.*

kind, it was prudent to draw a distinction between the wicked Whitehall bosses in their bowler-hats and the rest.

The Labour left was never in a position to do much direct damage with this simplistic critique. But its subterranean influence undoubtedly helped to soften up the public services for a more effective attack from the opposite flank. Margaret Thatcher's view of the senior civil service was formed before the comedy programmes *Yes, Minister* and *Yes, Prime Minister* hit the small screen (1981–7). But they provide a more accurate and vivid summary of her outlook than any book on the academic pseudo-theory of 'public choice', which uses lots of impressive jargon to say much the same thing. She regarded Britain's mandarins as inveterate empire-builders, whose chief priority was to increase their sphere of influence, swell their departmental budgets, and thus improve their standing in West-End clubs. Failing this, Whitehall culture demanded that they should fight with every available weapon to preserve their own patches. They would cooperate with ministers only so long as their interests coincided. Often this turned out to be the case, and right wingers were as scornful as the left whenever a Cabinet minister appeared to have 'gone native' — ie, preferred the advice of people who had accumulated years of relevant expertise after selection through competitive tests to 'the voice of the people' derived from the tabloid press and filtered through a motley crowd at Westminster.

When Mrs Thatcher came to office in 1979 she took immediate steps to put her theory into practice. The extent of her direct impact can be exaggerated; it was not true, for example, that every would-be Permanent Secretary was vetted in advance to ensure that he was 'one of us'. But it became pretty clear within Whitehall that one's chances of promotion would be improved by evidence of sympathy with Thatcherite ideas. The senior civil service was not 'politicised' so much as 'passified'. Instead of doing their proper job of using their greater expertise to identify possible pitfalls in proposed legislation, they tended to humour ministerial whims and pray that the consequences would not be too bad for the country and themselves. The *locus classicus* of this new understanding of civil service 'impartiality' was the Poll Tax — ridiculed within Whitehall one day, then foisted on the public as if the sceptics had never spoken.[8]

The success of 'public choice' theory in academia and politics is further evidence that contemporary liberalism has been hollowed-out. It is both superficial and self-contradictory. So it is hardly surprising that it has caught on in the British media and among politicians. Its crucial premise is that everyone acts out of perceived self-interest. If it made any sense to apply this theory to senior British civil servants in the late 1970s, their idea of self-interest must have been woefully short-sighted. It was hardly 'rational' to indulge in empire-building at a time when Britain was becoming increasingly difficult to govern. Instead of trying to take on more responsibilities, a 'rational actor' in those days would have put in for early retirement. But even if the theory really does help to explain the habits of the bureaucratic mind, it reveals much more about the motives of those who use it. If everyone acts out of self-interest, public choice theorists themselves must be selfish. Their low opinion of themselves makes them think they have the right to comment on their betters. When they try to persuade us to adopt their theories they can only do so to advance their personal interests. There might be a grain of truth in their thinking, and it might even prove helpful to the general public. But this happy outcome would be purely coincidental.

One logical inference from public choice theory is to abolish the state. Why trust bureaucrats with taxpayers' money, when the theory says that they love spending for its own sake? A less drastic alternative is to restrict their terms of office, so that they never get the chance to do too much damage. Senior posts could be filled by entrepreneurs on secondment, who will bring a much-needed dose of free market 'realism' to the public service before heading back to their parent company with a knighthood. Alternatively we could 'Bring Home the Revolution' by adopting the American system of bureaucracy, where all the top posts

---

[8]   See David Butler, Andrew Adonis and Tony Travers, *Failure in British Government: The politics of the poll tax*, Oxford University Press, 1994.

are captured by partisan figures and the whole guard can change whenever a president leaves office.

Since 1979 reform of the civil service has commenced along exactly these lines. Mrs Thatcher enticed a few businessmen into the bureaucracy.[9] Under Blair, Whitehall has been invaded by an army of special advisers and spin-doctors. They might not be needed for much longer, because many civil servants would now be perfectly willing to perform their functions, slowly rubbing out the old boundary between serving the state and working for the ruling party. After all, these are the working conditions which have prevailed for the last quarter of a century.

While Isaiah Berlin exaggerated the power of ideas, it would be equally mistaken to disregard their influence entirely. More exactly, if powerful people have stupid ideas, those around them will soon have to start behaving stupidly. It is hardly surprising that the vogue for public choice theory has given it an appearance of empirical validity. In our de-skilled civil service there is no longer any need to pose the question 'is he one of us'. 'He's whatever you want him to be' is the invariable answer. Once again ministers and civil servants are bound in a community of interest; but unlike the situation before 1979, the new imperative is to advance their own careers by presenting the results of departmental initiatives in the most favourable light. Along with impartiality, civil service anonymity is being eroded as ministers hunt for scapegoats when things go wrong. But while this development can have terrible consequences — witness the fate of Dr David Kelly — there are prizes to be gained for lying persuasively in front of a parliamentary select committee.

Whatever one thought of the old civil service, it was at least an integral part of Britain's liberal democracy. In the absence of a written constitution and formal separation of powers, civil servants (along with the judiciary) could see themselves as stumbling blocks in a system which could all too easily lapse into 'elective dictatorship'. It seems extraordinary that public choice

---

[9]   Very briefly, the present author had a job in the Inland Revenue after one of them, the late Lord Rayner of Marks and Spencer, had introduced administrative routines which damaged morale and deflected productive impulses into endless games of table-tennis.

theory should have been used in a conscious attempt to undermine the civil service, because its logic suggests that even if we
decide to keep the state we should certainly hedge governments
with as many checks and balances as possible. Instead, ministers
prattle on about 'joined-up government', defying their own theory which presupposes that Whitehall is full of briefcase-
wielding Hobbesians, consumed by a 'perpetual and restless
desire for power after power, which ceaseth only with death'.

Further down the hierarchy, ministers have found an inge-
nious way of confirming public choice theory. Thatcher, Major
and Blair have all been enthusiasts for selling off the state, on the
unproven assertion that public is bad and private good. But the
wholesale privatisation of government functions would remove
most of the incentive for being a minister; and in any case many
voters are still resistant to the idea. The real market has been held
back in specific areas, where its operations are simulated. Thus
schools, hospitals and GP practices are made to compete against
each other, to meet government targets or to make a decent pretence of doing so.

If this idea was intended to improve standards in the public
services, it was obviously doomed from the start. There is no
halfway house to a free market. But ministers like it, not least
because the creation of semi-autonomous agencies relieves them
from the danger of ever being held accountable for their decisions. Meanwhile, although the public services are free from
'real' market pressures, their local leaders can toast each other
with private-sector titles like 'Chief Executive'. Ironically they
now really do have a chance to build up petty principalities, as
public choice theory requires. All of the public services have
become encrusted with labyrinthine staff networks, most of
which would be scrapped if they only performed public service
functions. Thus even hospitals drag around a baggage-train of
publicists, logo-designers and human resource managers. Life
can be pretty good for middle managers in the public service; if
they are really lucky something newsworthy will happen under
their stewardship, in which case they might be suspended indef-
initely on full pay.

But the lower-ranking public servants are a different matter. If they were 'aspirational', they would not be working for limited rewards in the state sector. An index-linked pension might be held out as an inducement; but for young recruits it is a fairly distant one, while the assumptions of hollowed-out liberalism concentrate on short-term benefits. Job satisfaction cannot explain their career choice (except, perhaps, for members of the armed forces, whose training is geared towards a goal which public choice theorists understand pretty well). 'Vocation' has an insecure place in the lexicon of hollowed-out liberalism; it must be a pretentious word for a more down-to-earth motive. So why on earth do they do it?

The only explanation available to public choice theorists is that such people have no realistic alternative. It is safe to assume that they lack the necessary dynamism and skills to survive in the real world of supply and demand. They ought to be grateful to the state for offering them a livelihood, such as it is. Their enlistment as public servants implies a binding agreement to become the plaything of any government with bright reforming ideas. And yet they always seem to be complaining!

We have seen that the characteristic attitude of the hollowed-out liberal combines flattery with contempt. In their treatment of public servants, governments enjoy an unrestricted licence to indulge these natural inclinations. Contempt comes in a never-ending and ever-changing flow of paperwork from the centre. As public servants learn to conform to one set of directives, they are told to prepare themselves for another. To make sure that things are running smoothly, they are constantly subjected to appraisals by themselves and by under-qualified strangers. It is hardly surprising that the average social worker only has time to spend one hour out of seven in physical contact with society.

Even if public servants could escape from their bullying employers, they would still have to face over-demanding 'clients'. Many of them live under the threat of litigation even for excusable mistakes. According to one calculation, the compensation bill for schools would pay for 8,000 additional teachers, while claims against the National Health Service equate to the salaries of 22,700 nurses.[10] The average household pays £500 per year in taxes and insurance premiums to fatten the courtroom vultures. Teachers and medical staff sue, too, but maybe they have more reason. One teacher won £92,000 after spending two years at a London school where she was assaulted almost every day, 'attacked with a fire extinguisher, urinated on and twice hit so hard in the face that she lost teeth'.[11] The thugs who impose this rule by terror are usually the first to exploit our hollow culture of rights if any teacher retaliates. Public servants are given expensive counselling when they unexpectedly stumble into combat zones; the unfathomable logic of state largesse ensures that even people who have been specially trained for encounters with mayhem and murder are offered the same hollow consolation.

Meanwhile, the media justifies its most intrusive stories with the untenable argument that the private lives of public servants should be open to special scrutiny. Apart from the chances of compensation, now that we are ready to believe anything of anybody there is money to be made from selling false allegations of abuse to the press. Taken together, this working environment has driven many honest doctors and teachers to suicide or premature retirement on health grounds. At the same time, Harold Shipman evaded the incessant monitoring from above and below until more than two hundred people had perished at his hands.

For the last quarter century, ministers have been creating a regime in the public services which is guaranteed to generate avoidable mistakes. Yet much of the exhausting, error-inducing paperwork which confronts public servants is inspired by ministerial fears that the media will raise a hue and cry in the wake of an isolated blunder. The findings of public inquiries are invariably followed by an interview with an earnest politician, who will pledge that 'Nothing like this can ever happen again.' Systems will be changed. Additional bureaucrats will be hired to

[10] BBC News, 10 March 2004.
[11] *Times*, 7 April 2004.

police these systems. More public relations officers will be appointed to spin away the failings of the new procedures.

It must be acknowledged that some public inquiries can serve a constructive purpose in helping affected families to overcome bereavement. But in our contemporary context they have become even more futile than slamming the stable door after the horse has bolted. They are more like hiring a group of craftsmen to erect a set of impassable and elaborately-wrought gates while the rest of us set about demolishing the stable. The ensuing recommendations tend to be based on the assumption that systems are more important than the people who operate them, and that employees will have plenty of free time to do their jobs as well as attending endless seminars to familiarise them with the new, fool-proof 'mechanisms'.

While all this has been going on, political leaders have been pumping out the flattery, heaping praise on public sector workers as if they were exceptions to the general rule of selfishness. Somewhere deep down the politicians probably mean what they say. As we argued above, most of them are still fleshed-out liberals, who continue to prosecute their miserable trade in defiance of the evidence because they retain a sense of vocation. But their actions belie their words and contradict their feelings. Flattery might be powerful, but it can hardly convince long-suffering public servants that they are valued by their political gang-masters. It can, though, still serve a useful electoral purpose. Public servants like nurses, doctors and police remain highly popular with the voters — even with those who would willingly sue them at the first opportunity. A lyrical tribute at election-time will usually be enough to convince the electorate that the government is equally positive, whatever the tendency of its term-time activities, and that the opposition parties are only interested in power because they want the chance to be nice to the state's employees.

There must be times, during their sober moments of reflection, when our politicians wonder how they have managed to get away with their conduct towards the public services. Because the evidence suggests that they are still getting away with it in the most important quarters. A recent comprehensive survey of NHS staff found that forty percent had suffered 'work-related stress' in the preceding eighteen months. More than a third had been bullied or harassed by colleagues or patients; one in six had been physically attacked. In view of these deleterious distractions, it is hardly surprising that almost half 'had witnessed at least one error or near-miss which could have harmed a patient or colleague in the month before they answered the questions.' Yet in spite of all this, almost three-quarters still maintained that they were satisfied with their jobs.[12] Absenteeism is particularly serious within the NHS, which gives the press and politicians an opening for abuse. In some cases this does reflect a lack of commitment, but clinical depression and other psychological disorders can hardly be avoided when idealists run up against such a bleak reality.

Our politicians are probably so far gone that they will interpret these findings as proof of their hunch that most public servants are unemployable elsewhere. They must be making the best of a bad job because they have no other means of scraping a living. If so, the politicians would be wrong again. They have escaped the proper consequences of their behaviour towards public servants because the model of human motivation which has come to dominate political decision-making since 1979 is an unpleasant fiction. The public services have only survived because there are still plenty of people who continue to work for the state because they share the outlook of Philip Gould's father (if not his transcendent talents).

But we cannot take it for granted that this ethos will continue to survive against the odds. Can trained doctors stand out for long against the implied libel that they will only stir themselves to cure the sick under the twin stimuli of the cudgel and the carrot? An even greater threat is the present government's obsession with 'delivery'. Over time, the constant repetition of hideous jargon in their paperwork will persuade medical staff to regard their patients as nothing more than 'throughputs'. They might become so cynical that a death on the ward will one day be

[12] John Carvel in *Guardian*, 10 March 2004.

accepted as a 'completed' course of treatment. It seems that a tiny minority of health professionals has already begun to give death a hastening hand in order to free up much-needed bed-space.

Simultaneously, the integrity of the teaching profession has been under attack. In part, today's teachers are the victims of their over-optimistic predecessors, who built fantasies of social engineering into their support for comprehensive schools. Comprehensives were never going to produce equality of opp-ortunity, or anything like it. On rare occasions teachers can inspire a real revolution in the life-chances of their pupils. Much more often, they will find it impossible to transcend the child's home environment, and the influence of its peers. Well-meaning teachers were also at the forefront of campaigns to replace disci-plinary actions with the rational persuasion of recalcitrant chil-dren. In these respects, the beatings they have suffered have been inflicted with their own cane. But this does not excuse a succession of ministers of both parties, who have bullied teach-ers incessantly since the 1970s in obedience to the malevolent maxim that 'those who can, do; those who cannot, teach'.

As so often, New Labour is the worst offender here. Education is integral to any philosophy of social justice, which is why Tony Blair chose to make it the centrepiece of his sales-pitch in 1997. Certainly the existence of private schools is a greater affront to a fair society than the hobby of hunting. No house-points for guessing which of these practices the Blairites chose to counte-nance. They even betrayed their explicit promises to do away with selective state education. Instead of abolishing Tory league tables they have merely refined them, as if middle-class parents could be expected to send their children to schools which are producing decent results despite crippling handicaps, rather than the institution which can boast of the best record in absolute terms. There is another comic contradiction in the talk of paren-tal choice which is common to both main parties. If the post-war education system was half as bad as politicians' rhetoric sug-gests, few parents would be rational enough to be trusted with unlimited 'choice' in a matter which affects their children. Their behaviour certainly suggests that they learned logic in a 'failing' school. To secure a place in the 'best' schools, they will pay inflated prices for a house in the designated catchment area. They would hardly get an 'A' grade for honesty, either. To get into good religious schools they have no qualms about exaggerating the extent of their piety. At the same time, head teachers have a clear incentive to provide false information about the level of academic performance in their schools. If nothing is done to check these developments, the children of the best liars will be guaranteed a place at the school which has been most proficient in distorting its performance. This, we have to repeat, is the result of liberal thinking on education; or, more exactly, it is what happens when hollowed-out liberals inject their cruel absurdities into a system which was previously bedevilled by enfeebled philanthropists.

The present argument began with the case of Dr Katie Carr — well-meaning, dedicated to her work, and deeply confused. We suggested at the outset that Katie's profession placed her in a special category, and hopefully this is beginning to make some sense. Good teachers hate the idea that their efforts will be dissipated once their best pupils enter a world of adult injustices. Equally, good doctors want to restore unwell people to health. They tend to be excellent listeners and understand the relationship between the body and the mind, but they cannot hope to cure a perpetual flood of patients whose ailments stem from chronic unhappiness.[13]

Until recently, it would have been safe to say that conscientious teachers were the least enviable of public servants, given the difficulty of their work and the popular belief that long holidays leave them with nothing to complain about. But GPs are the new kids on the chopping-block. Everyone has it in for them. They are regarded as fair game by politicians, patients and the press. Yet most of them have only trained in the profession because they want to make a positive difference in the world.

---

[13] Contrary to the impression created by the popular television show, *Holby City*, in which no patient is allowed to leave the hospital without revealing their life-stories to members of staff.

They can easily be forgiven if the world ends up provoking a negative change in them.

In previous sections, we saw how this predicament has been landed upon us. The media and politicians now speak in a uniform language of hollowed-out liberalism. Yet these alien forces control the destiny of institutions which were created by very different liberals. We have suggested that the welfare state is a significant testament to the influence of 'positive' liberty. But it would be more accurate to say that it *was*, at the time of its inception. Liberals like Beveridge and Keynes were forceful advocates of human improvement. Beveridge's insurance schemes were devised as a fall-back for times of undeserved hardship for self-respecting individuals. When he identified idleness as one of the 'five giants' which he intended to slay, he was emphasising his hope that welfare institutions would do more than just keep people alive; they would also offer the sense of security which helps to underpin a purposeful existence. Other institutions, like the Arts Council which Keynes helped to establish, were devised in the immediate post-war period with the laudable intention of bringing the best products of Western culture within everyone's reach.

Thus the original welfare state was undoubtedly an instance where Berlin's 'positive' liberty and what we have called 'fleshed-out' liberalism coincided. But when we examine it today, we would have to conclude that the results have not measured up to the original idealism. Originally a means to an end, state welfare has long since lapsed into an end in itself. Its success, and that of any other government institution, is measured in terms of inputs and outputs, pounds, pennies and percentages — like any other 'low concern', as Burke would have put it. Beveridge and Keynes would not have disputed the importance of resources. But they anticipated other results, of no lesser value although they are impossible to quantify. They hoped that their efforts would improve the *attributes* of the British people. They did not want British elections to be won because a newspaper compared the Labour leader to a light-bulb; but equally they did not want the outcome to be decided because one party could promise to spend more money than its opponents. They hoped to create a situation in which politicians would be able to tell the public that spending was under control, because demand was restricted to the genuine cases of need which inevitably arise even in a 'rational' social order. The absence of progress in this respect is driven home to doctors, teachers, police and social workers, by the unhappy patients, unmanageable pupils, unruly revellers and irreconcilable partners who pass through their hands every day. Right-wingers of every party like to argue that these are the products of a 'dependency culture'. Rather, they are the castaways of consumerism — the ethos which was ushered into Britain in the wake of wartime solidarity. They are the victims of hollowed-out liberalism.

The idea that Britain was suffering from a 'dependency culture' was one of Mrs Thatcher's favourite cue-cards. It would be both trite and untrue to say that her remedies were worse than the disease. They were *identical* to the disease; they were the disease itself. Once upon a time poor deluded folk thought that a wound could only be healed by the weapon that had inflicted it. With the advent of Thatcher, the militant wing of hollowed-out liberalism was wheeled in to sort out the mess created by hollowed-out liberalism. The labels might have changed since 1979, but the principles are essentially the same.

Instead of helping to make life better, the welfare state is now exclusively concerned with preventing it from getting much worse. Even allowing for an element of real malingering, the swelling budgets of the welfare state are eloquent testimony to a growing list of genuine casualties. Fleshed-out liberals like Katie Carr only cheer up when they hear about an increase in the welfare budget (whether real, or the result of the government's creative accounting). They forget that every justifiable increase is a defeat for their ideals. They are worshipping a hollow institution, and only half-knowing it. Those who continue to defend the remnants of post-war social policy can only be commended; they have performed an heroic rearguard action in this respect, even if they have been forced to abandon most of their other positions. But just as criminals would encounter some difficulties if there were no honest people left to prey upon, without the public services which survive in Britain today the snake of hollowed-out liberalism would be deprived of its most nourishing food.

Since 1979, successive British governments have been killing off the public service ethos because they never believed it existed in the first place. It is hard to see how we can stop them. At least there are some signs of a shift from crude public choice theory. Professor Julian le Grand of the LSE, who has been working in the Downing Street Policy Unit, has argued that public servants are capable of disinterested endeavour, but that they are not immune from more mundane 'aspirations' for themselves and their families. On this view, governments must ensure that incentives have a creative rather than a corrosive effect. Although this seems like a typically bland Blairite exercise -- depicting the average public servant as a mixture of Philip Gould and his father -- at least the subject is being addressed by someone with a fertile mind and a place within government circles.[14]

It would be a mistake, though, to stake one's six-figure mortgage on the chances of the present government returning to sanity. Labour is now talking about bringing in the voluntary, charitable sector to supplement the efforts of public servants. As Alice Miles has noted, this idea was floated in the 1980s by thoughtful Tories, and came to nothing. This outcome was entirely predictable, since from the viewpoint of public choice the motives of voluntary workers are even less fathomable than those of state servants. Lurking behind the Tory idea was a distant echo of the Victorian ideal of charitable work performed by affluent spinsters with nothing better to do, or of generous donations from wealthy manufacturers who wanted to 'put something back' into the societies they had ravaged. Whatever the inspiration, the idea was ludicrous in the context of the 1980s, and makes no more sense now that Britons have 'Brought Home

---

[14]   See *New Statesman*, 16 October 2003.

the Revolution' and copied the American example of civic disengagement.[15]

In any case, politicians are less than half the problem. Although most of the electorate remains far more sensible than its representatives — and the 'rational voter' is imaginary — it would only take a modest minority of renegades to destroy the whole edifice. In a recent MORI poll more than three-quarters of respondents agreed that compensation claims are 'socially and morally responsible'.[16] Fortunately the findings are different when the question is more specific: nearly a half in the same poll said that they disliked the prospect of suing health professionals for negligence. But the combined polls suggest that up to a quarter of the public are ready to take the chance of cashing in, even on an innocent mistake, whenever they visit their doctor. This is not to say that Britain is about to 'Bring Home the Revolution' in this respect, duplicating the insanity of the US; or that when people claim compensation from the public services, naked material greed is always the predominant motivation. Yet even if we keep the dangers of a 'compensation culture' in perspective, we certainly live in a climate of complaint. We tolerate the existence of legal companies which promise 'No win, no fee', omitting to mention that if your claim does happen to win, the fee will be astronomical. The liberal snake has hissed in our ear that we can enjoy rights without acknowledging any responsibility to our fellow human-beings; and not even the most resolute of optimists can be surprised that some sad people have been converted by this self-serving argument.

Even if the compensation culture does not bankrupt the public services, the climate of complaint threatens to make it impossi-

---

[15] Alice Miles in *Times*, 19 May 2004, for evidence of decline in the British voluntary sector. The classic (though contested) work on this subject is Robert Puttnam, Bowling Alone: The Collapse and Revival of American Community, Touchstone edition, 2001.

[16] The 'compensation culture' is another incidence of 'victimless crime', where complainants clearly believe that no-one will suffer if their suit is successful. Even a hollowed-out liberal would have to protest that taxpayers have to foot the bill. Others will be more concerned with the impact on individuals who will have to live with their mistakes forever, even if they are cleared by a court.

ble for workers to maintain the necessary enthusiasm for the job. So how can they fight back? Concerted strike action to underline their grievances, at local or national level, would be a high-risk strategy. Whatever their real motive, threats of industrial action can be readily attributed to greed or callousness. As a general rule, the more valuable the public service the greater the difficulty of taking industrial action without losing moral support. Just as doctors tend to be sensitive people who are bound to be devastated by any threat of litigation, they are also the last people to contemplate a strike, even if they were trying to force a reduction in the paperwork which prevents them from doing the job they were trained for.

'Naming and shaming' is a less hazardous option. Again, this strategy could be adopted at local and national level, either by identifying specific individuals who are undermining public services, or by using the more responsible section of the media to appeal against general tendencies. There are signs that the teaching profession is beginning to take this option, pointing out that parents must take at least part of the blame for classroom indiscipline. But they are unlikely to be supported by the politicians. After all, parents have far more voting power than teachers.[17] This makes it unlikely that many public servants will be able to emulate the famous feat of Dr Richard Taylor at Wye Forest in 1997 (although one hopes that his remarkable victory on the single issue of private finance in his local hospital will encourage others to join the fray next time.)

If current trends continue, the most likely act of rebellion among public sector workers will be to do some voting of their own — with their feet. Key skilled professionals will decamp en masse into the private sector, leaving the politicians with plenty of league tables but no teams. No-one can blame health workers who sell their state-sponsored skills to the highest bidder at a time when loyalty is subjected to punishment rather than reward. This is already happening, of course, in an ad hoc fashion; vacancies are unfilled (particularly in the South-East, thanks

---

[17] Thanks to New Labour, of course, the parents will soon be joined by pupils in the virtual polling booths.

to the housing mania), while politicians struggle to entice into the country the very economic migrants who are attacked in the tabloid press as the parasitic harbingers of a mongrel nation.

The problem, of course, is that the abandonment of public service jobs might bring closer the very development which most public sector workers want to avoid – outright privatisation. Twenty-five years after Thatcher first took office, that word still provokes knee-jerk reactions. All 'serious' politicians have now accepted it: almost everybody else hates it. But taking the situation as a whole, can things really get much worse than the scandal of the post-code health lottery and the spectacular swindle of the PFI? I do not mean to say that individual public services will *improve* if they are privatised. Even Adam Smith recognised the proper limits of the profit motive. Rather, I am suggesting that when they get much worse in private hands a greater good might arise in reaction. To come over all Hegelian for a moment, it could be argued that the snake will only swallow its tail once Britain has been entirely hollowed-out. Since the ethos of public service remains the chief locus of resistance to the prevailing shallow ideas in Britain, we might think of letting it go in the hope that this would bring us back to sanity all the sooner. The NHS, all our places of learning, the prisons, the police, air-traffic control, the BBC and all the rest should be cast adrift in the market place; and those who work for them should give free rein to their 'aspirations' instead of struggling on with their present mixed motives. The resulting chaos would confront the politicians with the consequences of their actions over the last twenty-five years. Who knows? One of them might even start talking about '24 hours to save the NHS', and actually mean it.

But this is a counsel of despair which we might not have to heed. Ever since Marx's predictions about working-class immiseration ran into the brute fact that the 'proletariat' was actually getting more prosperous, his followers have continued to point out the absurdities of liberalism in the hope that it might implode for other reasons.[18] This style of prophesying is usually

---

[18] See, for example, Herbert Marcuse, *One Dimensional Man*, Routledge & Kegan Paul, 1964.

marred by its own contradictions. The typical argument goes: 'We have been sitting still while the world has gone to wrack and ruin, but if we resort to violence we can find the inner qualities to create a paradise on earth.'

We can hardly expect perfection to arise from the efforts of such imperfect people. Yet even if those wishful thinkers were wrong about our future prospects, we should not lightly dismiss the possibility that their diagnosis was right: that liberalism, as it has developed in the post-war world, is indeed riddled with absurdities which are getting far worse. A Cassandra like Herbert Marcuse, for example, found plenty of contradictions without witnessing overweight people paying hundreds of pounds to join a gymnasium, then trying to park as close as possible to the door to save themselves the trouble of walking. If the prophets of (short-term) doom were really onto something, then the longer we go on without changing our ways the more dramatic the transformation will have to be — unless we have reached the lamentable conclusion that human beings are doomed to be miserable and that the conquest of scarcity, the discovery of penicillin, the virtual disappearance of child mortality, etc etc, have merely given us more time on earth to brood about our inadequacies.

I would incline to a more positive view of our condition. Much of our current malaise, I would argue, arises from a healthy realisation that things should be so much better.[19] We will never be like Katie Carr's husband, either Mark I or II. We are wise enough to know that life will often be absurd and unhappy: but not *systematically* so, as it is at present.

If that is the case, then we should be ready to look around for explanations, instead of accepting the nonsense spewed at us by the media and the politicians. We have seen that even here there are tiny traces of better things. Sections of the tabloid press have realised that there is a market niche for more responsible journalism, and the internal discipline of political parties may be

---

[19]   Hence the success of New Labour's hollow 1997 theme song, which at best was a banal attempt to copy Clinton's use of Fleetwood Mac's genuinely-uplifting *Don't Stop*, and can now be played to serve the useful purpose of clearing any disco of Labour supporters who are now older and wiser.

cracking through over use. These developments give us reason to hope that when the snake of hollowed-out liberalism stops swallowing its tail, we might try to make something of our boasted values. The alternative is to subside into an era of well-meaning but right-leaning elective dictatorship in Britain, paving the way for our first exposure to totalitarian rule since Cromwell. Only a society of consumerist complacency could ignore the danger signs in the conduct of our present government. As long ago as 1741 David Hume warned that 'If any single person acquire power enough to take our constitution to pieces, and put it up a-new, he is really an absolute monarch'. Such a system, he thought, 'is the easiest death, the true *Euthanasia* of the BRITISH constitution'.[20] Oppressed, unhappy and confused as they are, fleshed-out liberals should dust down their copies of *On Liberty* and prepare for battle — on the understanding that this is likely to be their last chance to prove that Hume was wrong.

---

[20] David Hume, *Political Essays*, ed. Knud Haakonssen, Cambridge University Press, 1994.

Bibliography

Bellamy, Richard, *Liberalism and Modern Society*, Polity (1992).

Berlin, Isaiah, *Four Essays on Liberty*, Oxford University Press (1969).

Burke, Edmund, *Reflections on the Revolution in France*, Penguin edition (1969).

Butler, David, Adonis, Andrew, and Travis, Tony, *Failure in British Government: The politics of the poll tax*, Oxford University Press (1994).

Charlton, Bruce, and Andras, Peter, *The Modernization Imperative*, Imprint Academic (2003).

Cohen, Nick, *Pretty Straight Guys*, Faber and Faber (2003).

Crosland, Anthony, *The Future of Socialism*, abridged edition, Jonathan Cape (1964).

Elliott, Larry, and Atkinson, Dan, *The Age of Insecurity*, Verso (1998).

Figgis, Kate, *The Terrible Teens: What every parent needs to know*, Penguin (2004).

Freedland, Jonathan, *Bring Home the Revolution: How Britain can live the American dream*, Fourth Estate (1998).

Fromm, Erich, *Fear of Freedom*, Routledge edition (1960).

Fry, Stephen, *Paperweight*, Mandarin edition (1993).

Fukuyama, Francis, *The end of History and the Last Man*, Penguin edition (1992).

Galbraith, John Kenneth, *The Culture of Contentment*, Sinclair-Stevenson (1992).

Garnett, Mark, and Weight, Richard, *Modern British History: The essential guide*, Pimlico (2004).

Gould, Philip, *The Unfinished Revolution: How the modernisers saved the Labour Party*, Little, Brown (1998).

Graham, Gordon, *The Case Against the Democratic State*, Imprint Academic (2002).

Gray, John *Liberalism*, Open University Press (1986).

Gray, John, *Post-Liberalism: Studies in political thought*, Routledge (1996 edition).

Gray, John, *Al Qaeda and what it means to be modern*, Faber and Faber (2003).

Hazlitt, William, *Complete Works*, ed P.P Howe, Dent (1933).

Hobbes, Thomas, *Leviathan*, Blackwell edition (no date).

Hornby, Nick, *How to be Good*, Penguin (2001).

Hume, David, *Political Essays*, Cambridge University Press (1994).

Jenkins, Simon, *Accountable to None: The Tory nationalisation of Britain*, Hamish Hamilton (1995).

King, Anthony, et al, *Britain at the Polls 1992*, Chatham House (1992).

Mandeville, Bernard de, *The Fable of the Bees*, Pelican edition (1970).

Marcuse, Herbert, *One Dimensional Man*, Routledge & Kegan Paul (1964).

Mill, John Stuart, *Collected Works*, Routledge & Kegan Paul (1969).

O'Hara, Keiron, *Trust: From Socrates to Spin*, Icon (2004).

O'Neill, Onora, *A Question of Trust*, Cambridge University Press (2002).

Puttnam, Robert, *Bowling Alone: The collapse and revival of American community*, Touchstone edition (2001).

Rawls, John, *A Theory of Justice*, Oxford University Press (1972).

Rawnsley, Andrew, *Servants of the People: The inside story of New Labour*, Penguin edition (2001).

Rentoul, John, *Tony Blair: Prime Minister*, Little, Brown (2001).

Robertson, Geoffrey, *The Justice Game*, Vintage (1999).

Selbourne, David, *The Principle of Duty: An essay on the foundations of the civic order*, Sinclair-Stevenson (1994).

Shannon, Richard, *A Press Free and Responsible: Self-regulation and the Press Complaints Commission 1991-2001*, John Murray (2001).

Sutherland, Keith, *The Party's Over: Blueprint for a very English revolution*, Imprint Academic (2004).

Tregenza, Ian, *Michael Oakeshott on Hobbes: A study in the renewal of philosophical ideas*, Imprint Academic, 2003.

SOCIETAS

essays in political and cultural criticism

Vol.1   Gordon Graham, *Universities: The Recovery of an Idea*
Vol.2   Anthony Freeman, *God in Us: A Case for Christian Humanism*
Vol.3   Gordon Graham, *The Case Against the Democratic State*
Vol.4   Graham Allen MP, *The Last Prime Minister*
Vol.5   Tibor R. Machan, *The Liberty Option*
Vol.6   Ivo Mosley, *Democracy, Fascism and the New World Order*
Vol.7   Charles Banner/Alexander Deane, *Off with their Wigs!*
Vol.8   Bruce Charlton/Peter Andras, *The Modernization Imperative*
Vol.9   William Irwin Thompson, *Self and Society* (March 2004)
Vol.10   Keith Sutherland, *The Party's Over* (May 2004)
Vol.11   Rob Weatherill, *Our Last Great Illusion* (July 2004)
Vol.12   Mark Garnett, *The Snake that Swallowed its Tail* (Sept. 2004)
Vol.13   Raymond Tallis, *Why the Mind is Not a Computer* (Nov. 2004)
Vol.14   Colin Talbot, *The Paradoxical Primate* (Jan. 2005)
Vol.15   Alexander Deane, *The Great Abdication* (March 2005)
Vol.16   Larry Arnhart, *Darwinian Conservatism* (May 2005)

Contemporary public debate has been impoverished by two competing trends. On the one hand the increasing commercialization of the media has meant that in-depth commentary has given way to the ten-second soundbite. On the other hand the explosion of scholarly knowledge has led to such a degree of specialization that academic discourse has ceased to be comprehensible. As a result writing on politics and culture tends to be either superficial or baffling.

This was not always so—especially for politics. The high point of the English political pamphlet was the seventeenth century, when a number of small printer-publishers responded to the political ferment of the age with an outpouring of widely-accessible pamphlets and tracts. Indeed Imprint Academic publishes a facsimile reprints under the banner 'The Rota'.

In recent years the tradition of the political pamphlet has declined—with most publishers rejecting anything under 100,000 words. The result is that many a good idea ends up drowning in a sea of verbosity. However the digital press makes it possible to re-create a more exciting age of publishing. *Societas* authors are all experts in their own field, but the essays are for a general audience. Each book can be read in an evening.

The books are available retail at the price of £8.95/$17.90 each, or on bi-monthly subscription for only £5.00/$10.50.Full details:

www.imprint-academic.com/societas

EDITORIAL ADVISORY BOARD

IMPRINT ACADEMIC, PO Box 200, Exeter, EX5 5YX, UK
Tel: (0)1392 841600   Fax: (0)1392 841478   sandra@imprint.co.uk

SOCIETAS

essays in political and cultural criticism

The Party's Over
Keith Sutherland

200 pp., £8.95/$17.90, 0907845517

- 'This timely book examines why British politics has descended into the quagmire in which it now squirms.' *The Ecologist*

- 'An extremely valuable contribution – a subversive and necessary read.' **Graham Allen MP**, *Tribune*

- 'His analysis of what is wrong is superb … No one can read this book without realising that something radical, even revolutionary must be done.' **Sir Richard Body**, *Salisbury Review*

- 'Pithy, pungent, provocative — Keith Sutherland is becoming the Hazlitt of our age.' **Professor Robert Hazell**, Director, The Constitution Unit, UCL

- 'Anyone who is concerned about the serious lack of interest in the parliamentary system should read this book.' **Lord Weatherill**, Speaker of the House of Commons (1983–1992)

Consider the following paradox: As the leaders of both of the main British political parties subscribed to the neoconservative doctrine on Iraq, everybody else in the birthplace of parliamentary democracy was effectively disenfranchised. Yet one of the rationales supporting the deployment of UK forces in Iraq was the wish to export democracy to the Middle East. The Emperor would appear to have mislaid his clothes.

Judging by the lack of ministerial resignations in the wake of the Butler enquiry, Britain is no longer a *parliamentary* democracy. The classical doctrine of joint and several ministerial responsibility is revealed to be a fiction, and Lord Hailsham's verdict of 'elective dictatorship' is a better assessment of the British constitution. By contrast unelected bodies like the BBC are now far more accountable for their actions. The reason of this paradox is the monopoly power of the ruling party, controlled by the Prime Minister.

The UK political party started off as a loose association of like-minded MPs. However, in recent years the tail has been firmly wagging the dog — politicians now have no alternative but to choose and then fall in line behind a strong leader with the charisma to win elections. This book examines the historical forces that gave rise to the modern political party and questions its role in the post- ideological age. If we all now share the liberal market consensus, then what is the function of the party?

The book argues that the tyranny of the modern political party should be replaced by a mixed constitution (*politeia*) in which the phrase 'Her Majesty's Government' is restored to its original meaning, advocacy is entrusted to a true aristocracy of merit, and democratic representation is achieved via a (selective) jury-style lottery. Keith Sutherland is publisher, *History of Political Thought*; his previous books include *The Rape of the Constitution?* (2000).

sample chapters, reviews and TOCs: **www.imprint-academic.com/societas**

The Case Against the Democratic State
Gordon Graham

We are now so used to the state's pre-eminence in all things that few think to question it. This essay contends that the gross imbalance of power in the modern state is in need of justification, and that democracy simply masks this need with an illusion of popular sovereignty. Although the arguments are accessible to all, it is written within the European philosophical tradition. The author is Professor of Moral Philosophy at the Uniiversity of Aberdeen. 96 p., £8.95/$17.90

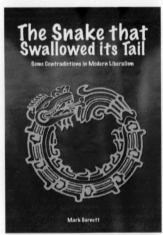

The Snake that Swallowed its Tail
Mark Garnett

Liberal values are the hallmark of a civilised society. Yet they depend on an optimistic view of the human condition, Stripped of this essential ingredient, liberalism has become a hollowed-out abstraction. Tracing its effects through the media, politics and the public services, the author argues that hollowed-out liberalism has helped to produce our present discontent. Unless we stop boasting about our values and try to recover their essence, liberal society will be crushed in the coils of its own contradictions. 96 pp., £8.95/$17.90

The Modernization Imperative
Bruce Charlton & Peter Andras

Modernisation gets a bad press in the UK, and is blamed for the dumbing down of public life. But modernisation is preferable to lapsing back towards a static, hierarchical society. This book explains the importance of modernisation to all societies and analyses anti-modernisation in the UK—especially such problems as class divisions, political short-termism and the culture of spin.

96 pp., £8.95/$17.90

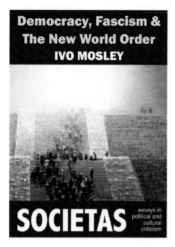

Democracy, Fascism and the New World Order
Ivo Mosley

Growing up as the grandson of the 1930s blackshirt leader, made Ivo Mosley consider fascism with a deep interest. Whereas conventional wisdom sets up democracy and fascism as opposites, to ancient political theorists democracy had an innate tendency to lead to extreme populist government, and provided demagogues with the opportunity to seize power. This book argues that totalitarian regimes can be the outcome of unfettered mass democracy. 96 pp., £8.95/$17.90

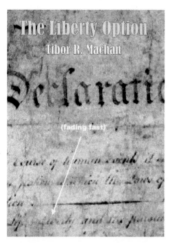

The Liberty Option
Tibor R. Machan

This book advances the idea that for compelling moral and practical reasons it is the society organised on classical liberal principles that serves justice best, leads to prosperity and encourages the greatest measure of individual virtue. The book contrasts the Lockean ideal with the various statist alternatives, defends it against its communitarian critics and lays out some of its policy implications. Machan is a research fellow at Stanford University. His books include *Classical Individualism* (Routledge, 1998). 104 pp., £8.95/$17.90

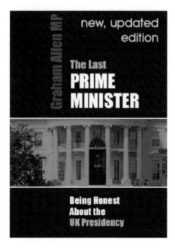

The Last Prime Minister
Graham Allen MP

Echoing Gandhi, Graham Allen thinks the British constitution would be a very good idea. In *The Last Prime Minister* he showed the British people how they had acquired an executive presidency by stealth. This timely new edition takes in new issues, including Parliament's constitutional impotence over Iraq.

'Well-informed and truly alarming.' **Peter Hennessy**

'Iconoclastic, and well-argued, it's publication could hardly be more timely.' **Vernon Bogdanor, THES**

96 pp. £8.95/$17.90

sample chapters, reviews and TOCs: **www.imprint-academic.com/societas**